LIFE IN CHRIST

LIFE IN CHRIST

Edward Donnelly

BRYNTIRION PRESS

Cover design:
Evangelical Press, Darlington

Published by Bryntirion Press
Bryntirion, Bridgend CF31 4DX, Wales, UK

Printed by Gomer Press, Llandysul, Ceredigion SA44 4JL

Dedicated with affection to
the Christians of Wales and
from further afield
who meet in conference
at Aberystwyth each summer

*'As for the saints in the land,
they are the excellent ones,
in whom is all my delight.'*
(Psalm 16:3)

Contents

Preface

THE messages on which most of this book is based were first preached in Aberystwyth on the west coast of Wales. It was August 2001, the week of the English Conference organised by the Evangelical Movement of Wales, and my wife and I still look back with gratitude on those golden days.

It was a time of unbroken and delightful fellowship. The town was full of Christians, and a 'walk' along the promenade could take hours, with friends to greet and talk to every few yards. There was a peculiar gentleness and joy in the atmosphere and many of us found that our hearts were unusually tender. This was in great measure the effect of the presence among us of the Holy Spirit, blessing us with that unity which the psalmist describes as 'like the dew of Hermon, which falls on the mountains of Zion' (Ps. 133:3). Where on this earth would a believer rather be than among so many of the Lord's people?

The sense of God's presence was particularly evident in the meetings in the Great Hall of the University. I had the daunting privilege (both words equally apt) of preaching each morning and, as I did so, something happened. My pedestrian and unremarkable treatment of our subject, over which I had been fretting in the bleak hours before delivering the first message, seemed to take wings as it passed from me to well over a thousand eager listeners. The sermons somehow became more cogent and powerful than they had been when I prepared them. Why the improvement? Because of the people to whom I was speaking and the fact that the Spirit was honouring their faith. For they had prayed, for months, some of them, that the Lord would bring home his Word to their hearts. They had come to the conference with an appetite for spiritual food and were now looking at me expectantly. No preacher worthy of the name could fail to be lifted above himself when faced with such a gathering. Even yet I thank God for those of you who were there, 'that when you received the word of God, which you heard from us, you accepted it not as the word of men but as what it really is, the word of God, which is at work in you believers'(1 Thess. 2:13).

As I sit now at the computer, there is no congregation in front of me and once again the words seem to limp instead of running. Set down in cold black and white, something vital appears to be missing. But God's Word is always living and active, whether spoken or written, and, as Charles Spurgeon used to remind himself, 'I believe in the Holy Spirit.' So I have tried to transfer the sermons to the printed page in the confidence that God will own his truth, and that any attempt at exposition, no matter how stumbling, is warranted by the greatness of the theme before us—'Life in Christ', the essence of our faith.

EDWARD DONNELLY
April 2007

Introduction

To be a Christian is to be related to Jesus Christ. But in what way? Does admiring him and trying to live as he did make you a Christian? Not according to the Bible, which nowhere holds out the possibility of salvation by imitation. What about worshipping him as a divine being? Since he is fully divine, he certainly deserves and calls for your worship, and no one is a Christian for whom Jesus is not Lord and God. But to bow in reverence before him is not enough. You need to understand that Christ came to earth to live and die in the place of sinners like yourself—and then to trust him as your Saviour, depending entirely for your acceptance with God on him and what he has done for you. This is what it means to become a Christian, for it is only the person who 'believes in him' who has 'eternal life' (John 3:16).

Saving faith brings us into a relationship which has many facets, thrillingly rich and full of joyful surprises. We come to know the Saviour as our master and Lord, our priest and king, our friend and our brother. But the New Testament has a favourite description of our connection with Christ. It has been strangely neglected in the church, and you may not be in the habit of thinking of yourself in this way. The idea is mysterious and profound, yet at the same time simple to grasp. When we understand it, our lives are transformed, and one purpose of this book is to build it securely into the consciousness of those of you who are Christians. Even more importantly, I am praying that what I have to say will awaken a longing for the Lord

Jesus in those of you who are not yet believers—so keen a desire for this most intimate of relationships that you will not stop searching until God has made Christ himself a living reality for you.

What is this connection? Theologians call it 'union with Christ'. The apostle Paul expresses it by means of the preposition 'in'. Such a little word for something so inexpressibly wonderful! So prominent is the idea in his thinking that he uses the phrase 'in Christ', and others such as 'in him' or 'in the Lord', nearly two hundred times in his writings. In the first fourteen verses of his letter to the Ephesians, for example, he writes of being 'in' Christ no fewer than eleven times, beginning with his introductory description of his readers. The believers in that city and district are the 'faithful in Christ Jesus' (Eph. 1:1). Similarly, the Philippians are 'the saints in Christ Jesus' (Phil. 1:1) and the Colossians are 'the saints and faithful brothers in Christ' (Col. 1:2). For Paul, a Christian is simply a man or woman 'in Christ'. No wonder, then, that union with Christ has been called 'the central truth of the whole doctrine of salvation',[1] lying 'at the heart of evangelical theology'.[2]

Union with Christ is so fundamental that it transcends time and space, stretching from before the creation of the universe into the endless ages of the world to come. The doctrine is vast in its dimensions and includes within itself all the blessings of redemption. Although some of the greatest Christian minds have explored it, no one has ever come close to mastering it. So please do not expect a comprehensive discussion from me! As I have reflected on it, I feel like a child paddling on the shore of an unfathomable ocean. But the ground beneath my feet has been reassuringly solid, and this truth has, I think, changed me for the better. So I hope that you will find, as you read, that you can say with confidence that you are 'in' the Lord Jesus Christ and that this will come to mean more to you than ever before.

We will see how union with Christ provides us with a new identity and will learn how to draw directly from him the strength to live Christlike lives in this fallen world. We will be reminded of the worldwide family to which we now belong. We will come to understand how pain and suffering are God's paradoxical means of bringing us closer to Jesus and making us more like him.

But we begin with the way in which we consciously enter into union with the Lord.

1
Believing into Christ

Who is this Christ to whom believers are united? He is the eternal Son of God, the same in substance and equal in power and glory with the Father. He is the Messiah, the Anointed One, the fulfilment of the ancient hope of Israel. He is the Saviour, who lived a sinless life, died on a cross, was raised from the dead and has ascended into heaven. He is the present King and the coming Judge of the universe. All this and more. But we are going to focus on two phrases, particularly the first, used by Paul when he describes Jesus Christ as 'the last Adam' and 'the second man' (1 Cor. 15:45,47).

The last Adam

At this point I want you to use your imagination. Picture two giants—immense, towering figures. Each is wearing around his waist a broad leather belt, and on that belt are millions of tiny hooks, with a human being hanging from each hook. Every human who has ever lived, is living now or will live in the future, is hanging from the belt of one or other of these giants. The name of one giant is Adam and the name of the other Christ.

I know! It does sound a weird illustration, particularly in what is supposed to be a serious book. So let me re-assure you. It does not come from some gimmicky collection of 'Sermon Aids for Busy Preachers', but from the massively learned and utterly earnest Thomas Goodwin, a leading Puritan theologian. In his treatise, 'Christ Set Forth', when discussing Paul's description of Jesus Christ as the last Adam in 1 Corinthians 15, he writes:

> Adam . . . was reckoned as a common public person, not standing singly or alone for himself, but as representing all mankind to come of him . . . [Paul] speaks of them [Adam and Christ] as if there had never been any more men in the world, nor were ever to be for time to come, except these two. And why?

Then comes the illustration:

> Because these two between them had all the rest of the sons of men hanging at their girdle.[3]

Can you visualise it? Here are the two giants and the two belts, or 'girdles', with every human being hanging (the hooks are my addition, but they must have been hanging from something!) from one or the other. And Goodwin is using this far-fetched but undeniably vivid picture to illustrate what is called 'covenant theology'. This is the teaching that God deals with humanity not primarily as isolated individuals but as a body or group, by means of a divinely imposed arrangement called a covenant.

In a covenant, God appoints one person to act on behalf of many, as their representative or covenant head. Whatever the relationship of the head with God may be, that is counted as the relationship also of every individual whom they represent. All God's dealings with the many are through the one. He has appointed only two such representatives—Adam and Christ—and every human being is represented by either one or the other. You can understand your problem and your need as a sinner only by realising that you were born in Adam and so are represented by him.

You can understand and rejoice in salvation only by recognising that it means being taken out of Adam and brought into Christ, so that he becomes your new representative. Paul expands on this in Romans 5:12-21.

'One man'

The key phrase in the passage in Romans 5 is 'one man'. Everything that Adam, the 'one man', did is counted as having been done also by everyone he represents. *His* relationship with God is counted, or 'reckoned', as being *their* relationship. In the same way, everything that Christ, the 'one man', did is counted to the credit of those he represents, and all that he was in his obedience and purity is regarded as theirs.

We can see at once how this works out in practice. All mankind is trapped in a web of sin and death. 'None is righteous, no, not one . . . for all have sinned and fall short of the glory of God' (Rom. 3:10,23). Why is that so? Is it simply because every single individual happens to have chosen, quite independently, to sin? No! says Paul. It is because of the sin of Adam, our covenant head. The apostle makes this point seven times in eight verses, so frequently that we cannot miss it:

> sin came into the world *through one man* . . . many died through *one man*'s trespass . . . the result of that *one man*'s sin . . . the judgement following *one trespass* . . . because of *one man*'s trespass, death reigned . . . *one trespass* led to condemnation for all men . . . by the *one man*'s disobedience the many were made sinners.
>
> (verses 12,15,16,17,18,19)

Do you grasp the force of his emphasis? 'The one man'! It is not merely a coincidence that all are sinners. It is not a fluke or a bizarre statistical anomaly that every human

17

being, apart from the uniquely born Jesus of Nazareth, happens to have disobeyed. It is because of our relationship with Adam. As the Westminster Shorter Catechism puts it: 'all mankind, descending from him [Adam] by ordinary generation, sinned in him, and fell with him, in his first transgression'.[4] All were hanging from the giant's belt. When the giant sinned, we sinned, and when the giant fell, we fell to death and judgement. Sin is the universal human condition because of our union with Adam.

And yet, thank God, that is not the end of the story. For there is salvation, a promise of abundant life and blessing. But how does this salvation come? In what way can a person receive it? It is here that Paul displays especially profound biblical insight. One of his longest-running controversies, and it is in his mind here, was with those who argued that people are saved by the good things they do, by trying their best, by their 'works'. Their view of salvation was of God setting millions of single examination papers, as it were, one for each person. Each individual has to sit the exam for himself or herself, and it is up to the candidate whether he or she passes or fails. If they do well enough, achieve a sufficiently high mark, they will pass and be saved.

But, says Paul, is that how we were lost in the first place? No!—'through one man'. We were lost because of our representative, Adam. So how are we going to be saved? In exactly the same way as we were lost—'through one man', through our covenant representative, for 'Adam . . . was a type of the one who was to come' (v.14). So, beginning in verse 15, he again stresses this truth:

the free gift by the grace of that *one man* Jesus Christ abounded for many . . . reign in life through the *one man*

. . . *one act* of righteousness leads to justification and life for all men . . . by the *one man*'s obedience the many will be made righteous.

(verses 15,17,18,19)

Do you see the majestic symmetry of it all, how this reflects the mind of the all-wise God, who knows the end from the beginning and has planned everything in perfect wisdom? We are saved in the same way as we were lost. Our redemption, though infinitely greater than our ruin, is in this respect parallel to it. In Adam we sinned. In Adam we fell. In Adam we were condemned. In Adam we died. And then in Christ we obeyed. In Christ we lived a perfect life. In Christ we paid for sin. In Christ we have been raised. In Christ we live for ever. All that he is is counted as ours. All that he suffered is counted as ours. All that he achieved is counted as ours.

This is what Goodwin meant when he wrote, 'these two between them had all the rest of the sons of men hanging at their girdle'. George Smeaton agrees: 'So fully are all the individuals represented by that one man, that we may say there have been but two persons in the world, and but two great facts in human history.'[5] Or as Paul puts it in 1 Corinthians 15:22, 'For as in Adam all die, so also in Christ shall all be made alive.' You and I belong to the one head or the other, and whether ultimately we die or live depends on our representative. So we can understand now what Paul means when he calls the Saviour 'the last Adam . . . the second man'. He is the head of a new humanity, the leader of a new species of men and women who are in a new relationship with God and are being dealt with by God on an entirely new basis.

We now have a new head, a new covenant representative. We are joined to 'the second man'. He is called 'second' because, praise God, there are many more new men and women to come—millions of them, 'a great multitude that no one could number' (Rev. 7:9). But the hymn-writer was mistaken in saying that

> *When all was sin and shame,*
> *A second Adam to the fight*
> *And to the rescue came.*[6]

For Christ is never referred to in the Scriptures as the second Adam. He is (and it should make us want to shout and sing) the 'last' Adam—the final, the perfect, the ultimate Adam, the supreme representative who has once and for all accomplished salvation.

This is the Saviour in whom we are called to believe. Union with Christ means becoming part of God's new beginning for the human race.

The great transfer

We can think of salvation, then, as being unhooked from Adam's belt and hooked onto Christ's. This is a change so radical, a transaction so momentous, that it must be the work of God himself. Those who are saved are now represented before him by a new covenant head and have been transferred into an entirely different category of being. Salvation is, in fact, union with Christ. The effecting of this transfer is the work in particular of God the Holy Spirit, whom theologians have described as 'the bond of union'. He it is who joins us to the Saviour, who brings us out of Adam and places us in Christ. As Paul puts it when writing of the unity of the church, 'in one Spirit we were all baptized into one body' (1 Cor. 12:13).

How does this happen? What is the essential, unmistakable evidence that God the Spirit is joining someone to

God the Son? It is the exercise of faith. In the words of the Shorter Catechism, 'The Spirit applieth to us the redemption purchased by Christ'—in other words, brings us into saving contact with that redemption—'*by working faith in us, and thereby uniting us to Christ*'.[7] In regenerating us, he enables us to believe in Jesus and, from our perspective, this is the crucial element in becoming a Christian. It is by faith that we enter Christ, and until we exercise faith we are not 'in him'.

There is a degree of mystery here, and we must be careful not to try to force the Scriptures into the constricting boundaries of our inadequate human logic. For, from one viewpoint, God's elect people have always been in Christ. God 'chose us in him before the foundation of the world' (Eph. 1:4). Just before he went to the cross, the Lord Jesus prayed to the Father for 'the people whom you gave me out of the world' (John 17:6). All those who would later believe belonged to Christ in eternity, therefore, and he considered them as having been given to him long before he died to obtain forgiveness for their sins. So there is a sense in which all Christians have been in Christ since before the beginning of time.

We do not, however, enter into this union or experience its benefits until we actually believe. Paul could remind the same Ephesians who had been 'chosen before the foundation of the world' of a time when they had not been in Christ but in Adam—'by nature children of wrath . . . separated from Christ' (Eph. 2:3,12). Similarly, in the middle of a list of greetings to the believers in Rome, he says of two of his relatives, Andronicus and Junia, 'they were in Christ before me' (Rom. 16:7). At one time they had been in Christ, but he had not. The reason was not that he had not been chosen by God, but because he had not yet come to faith. Believing is the essential link. 'For God so loved the world, that he gave his only Son, that whoever'—of the people of Adam, lost, doomed and wretched—'believes in him should not perish but have eternal life' (John 3:16).

Believing in Christ

But what does it mean to believe? We believe facts. The first fact I was taught in history class at grammar school was that the battle of Bosworth Field, where Henry Tudor gained the throne of England, took place in 1485. I believed it. In geography I believed, because so I was told, that Lima is the capital of Peru. I still believe those facts, but I cannot say that they challenge or move me. They have never made my heart sing or filled me with wonder as I think of them. I have never wakened my wife in the middle of the night so that she can rejoice with me over the identity of the Peruvian capital. Not once have I asked myself what impact the battle of 1485 is making on my life. I understand these things intellectually and hold them to be true, but they make absolutely no difference to how I behave or feel.

Is this what we mean when we speak of believing in Christ? Are we simply talking about mental assent, intellectual understanding? Of course not! To believe in Christ is far more than agreeing that he existed and that he suffered in the place of sinners. It is to be hooked to Christ's belt, to be one with him for ever. It implies absolute commitment, total identification. If you believe in Christ, you depend on him. 'Depend' is the appropriate word, because it comes from the Latin 'to hang from', which is exactly what you do. You hang upon Christ. You look to him for all things. You are his, body and soul, for time and for eternity. He is everything to you; you have transferred to him your allegiance. You have cast in your lot with him, and your everlasting destiny is inextricably linked with him. You are now inside him. In him you find your new identity.

Think of the first disciples—what did believing involve for them? It was nothing less than a revolution in their lives. From now on they were men totally committed to Jesus. They identified themselves with him publicly. They listened to him and talked with him. Whatever he told them they believed and tried to obey. He and they walked the roads of Palestine and slept under the stars together. They worked together and were persecuted together. They were one with him and stood with him. For them, believing meant the giving of themselves irrevocably to the Lord so that they were his men for ever. In Peter's words, 'we have left everything and followed you' (Matt. 19:27).

When we first come to faith, we may not realise how all-embracing is the commitment we have made or what Christ may ask from us. A young bridegroom does not fully understand on his wedding day just how much his life is about to change. His bachelor days have gone once and for all. The beautiful woman, on whom he is gazing so fondly, has plans for him. She will want to take some of the money which he previously devoted to hobbies and sport and fritter it away on food and housekeeping. Watching three hours of football on television may not be her idea of a perfect evening. Many hitherto unrecognised areas of self-centredness in his life are going to be exposed and challenged. He will have to learn in a thousand ways what it means to live for another person. But, although he does not yet understand the dimensions of his commitment, it is all there in essence—permanent, total, all-absorbing, for better or worse, for richer or poorer, in sickness and in health. And such is our commitment to Christ.

The anaemic version of faith which is being peddled in so many quarters today is a travesty, a soul-destroying distortion. People are told that long ago, in some undefined way, Christ died for their sins at Calvary and that all that they have to do is agree that he did this and accept the fact that his sacrifice was offered on their behalf. This, they are informed, is saving faith—all that is necessary to become a Christian. It is rather like someone massively in debt who one day hears good news from their bank manager. A distant relative has been kind enough to pay off all that they owe. All they need to do is turn up at the bank, sign a form and, hey presto, their debts are cancelled. It might be polite to send a thank-you note to their benefactor, but they do not need to meet or have anything further to do with the person who has helped them in this way. It is simply a matter of understanding what has been done for them by someone else and accepting it.

But saving faith in the Bible is so utterly different. It is active, dynamic, committed. The New Testament talks about believing 'in' Christ or 'into' him or 'upon' him, and there is movement and connection in these significant prepositions. Above all, an intensely personal relationship is involved, a living union with the Son of God. Faith is coming to Christ, receiving Christ, trusting Christ. It is described as eating his flesh and drinking his blood (John 6:53). Faith means entering him, belonging to him, being one with him, being joined to him for ever. Saving faith is not receiving the benefits of a remote, impersonal transaction by someone we never meet and do not know. It means, rather, being able to say, 'to me to live is Christ' (Phil. 1:21).

This is why the scriptural analogies of union with Christ are so intimate. We are the stones in the building and he is the cornerstone (Eph. 2:19-22; 1 Pet. 2:4-8); we are the branches and he is the vine (John 15:1-8); we are the members of the body and he is the head (Eph. 4:15-16; 1 Cor. 12); he is the husband and we are the wife (Eph. 5:30,32). The relationship is personal, close, mutually involved. It is having a Christ who is near, who is one with us.

One of the implications of this truth is that salvation is a much bigger transaction than many people realise. It is certainly not something that we can understand or explain in a purely man-centred way, for it is more than simply our making a decision. How could a mere act of our wills transform our standing before God? When we seek to understand salvation, we have to see it primarily as God's plan and God's doing, as an immense miracle of grace. It means being caught up by divine power and transferred into a new, everlasting relationship of unity and loyalty, so that Jesus Christ is our all in all. Salvation is being transferred from Adam to Christ.

The new relationship

What difference does being 'in Christ' make? For Paul, the difference is total: 'Therefore, if anyone is in Christ, he is a new creation. The old has passed away; behold, the new has come' (2 Cor. 5:17). Our relationship with God has been revolutionised. Previously, we were 'in Adam' and therefore alienated from our Maker, under his wrath and destined for condemnation. But now his dealings with us are always and entirely through Christ, for he never interacts with the believer in any other way. Every word he speaks to us—every command, every gracious promise, every rebuke or instruction—is through Christ. Every blessing we receive is through Christ. Every fatherly chastisement is through Christ. Every time God preserves us, strengthens us, guides or helps us—all is through Christ.

The Greek language has a preposition *sun*, which means 'together with'. It has passed over into English as 'syn-' or 'sym-' in words such as synergy, symphony, sympathy and so on. Paul likes to take this preposition and add it as a prefix to Greek verbs. Some of these compounds are not found anywhere else and it may be that he has made them up! But it is because of his eagerness to express the degree and scope of our union with Christ.

He tells us, for example, that we suffer with him (Rom. 8:17); are crucified with him (Rom. 6:6); die with him (2 Tim. 2:11); are buried with him (Rom. 6:4); are made alive with him (Eph. 2:5); are raised with him (Col. 3:1); take on the same form with him (Phil. 3:10); are glorified with him (Rom. 8:17); live with him (Rom. 6:8); sit with him (Eph. 2:6); reign with him (2 Tim. 2:12). With him! Always with him! Christ is 'our wisdom and our righteousness and sanctification and redemption' (1 Cor. 1:30). We are 'enriched in him' (1 Cor. 1:5). God 'has blessed us in Christ with every spiritual blessing in the heavenly places' (Eph. 1:3).

Our prayers are answered only because of our union with Christ, because the Lord Jesus made clear the condition for successful praying: 'If you abide *in me*, and my words abide in you, ask whatever you wish, and it will be done for you' (John 15:7). In other words, our unity with him is so profound that the believer's prayers are in fact echoes of the holy desires of Christ himself. How wonderful! What a light it casts on what is really happening when we kneel in God's presence! Robert L. Dabney comments:

Each gracious affection is a feeble reflex of the same affection, existing, in its glorious perfection, in our Redeemer's heart. As when we see a mimic sun in the pool of water on the earth's surface, we know that it is only there because the sun shineth in his strength in the heavens. How inexpressible the comfort and encouragement arising from this identity of affection! . . . Does the believer have . . . a genuine and spiritual aspiration for the growth of Zion? Let him take courage; that desire was only born in his breast because it before existed in the breast of His head, that Mediator whom the Father heareth always.[8]

Realising this, can your praying ever be the same again?

Our union with Christ is so all-embracing that it includes our physical flesh, our bodily organs, for they too have become part of Christ. Paul makes this clear when he writes to the Corinthians that for believers to misuse their bodies in sexual immorality is to 'take the members of Christ and make them members of a prostitute' (1 Cor. 6:15).

It is a startling expression, is it not? None of us perhaps would have dared to go so far. But how striking that the inspired apostle, dealing with earthy, shameful physicality, finds the motivation for avoiding sin in the mysterious union between Jesus and his people! Christ himself is involved somehow when you or I sin. We are joined to him so closely that we take him with us into disobedience. What more persuasive reason do we need for resisting temptation? 'Do you not know', asks Paul, 'that your bodies are members of Christ? Shall I then take the members of Christ and make them members of a prostitute? Never!'

Sinclair Ferguson emphasises the personal intimacy of the relationship when he writes that the blessings of redemption ought not to be viewed as merely having Christ as their ultimate causal source but as being ours only by direct participation in Christ.[9]

He is pointing to a common flaw in our thinking. We know, of course, that Jesus Christ is the source of all our blessings. But 'ultimate' can make us think of someone far away, and we can tend to suppose that there is a distance between the Lord himself and the blessings he has for us. 'Of course he purchased them', we say. 'We owe them all to him. They are stored, as it were, in a safe deposit or treasure chest, and because of what he has done for us we can come by faith, open the chest and take out the blessings.' But that is not at all the way in which these gifts become ours. Instead, we should see ourselves as coming to the Lord Jesus Christ himself, or, rather, as being part of Christ himself, and receiving each blessing from his own hand as he reaches it to us.

Everything in this life for which you have reason to be grateful is yours only because you are in him. Forgiveness, righteousness, growth in holiness, guidance, peace of conscience and joy in the Holy Spirit—all come from the Lord Jesus. 'By direct participation in Christ.' Never forget it! When Luther said, 'I will have nothing to do with an absolute God', he meant that he could relate to God the Father only through Christ. Similarly, we enjoy no blessing 'absolutely'. Every one of them, without exception, is received directly from our Saviour.

Calvin puts it beautifully and so simply (Why do people think John Calvin is complicated?):

We are enriched in Christ, because we are members of his body, and we have been ingrafted into him; and, furthermore, since we have been made one with him, he shares with us all that he has received from the Father.[10]

What a wonderful expression! 'He shares with us all that he has received from the Father.' This is what our new relationship means. An awareness of this reality will keep us from spiritual 'cupboard love', that immaturity which values the gifts more than the Giver. For they cannot be separated. To enjoy the blessings we must be constantly in the posture of dependent trust in the One in and from whom they are to be experienced.

Should we not then love Jesus Christ? Should our hearts not go out to him now in gratitude and worship?

In Christ for ever
And what security this provides for the Christian! That is the great point of Paul's discussion in Romans 5. He has been speaking of being justified through faith, of peace, assurance and rejoicing, and he wants to confirm all that, to bring home to the hearts of his readers that their salvation is certain and sure. He does it in a strange, yet persuasive, way, by reminding them of the utter inevitability of the results of being in Adam.

What is the universal fact of human existence? Death. What is the ultimate destiny of every single person? To die. Is there any possibility of escaping death? No. Are there any exclusions, exceptions, people in a special category? No. Why is that so? Because we are all in Adam and it is absolutely certain that all who are in Adam will die.

So what does this mean for those who have been taken out of Adam and placed in Christ? There is the same certainty and inevitability. What is the universal fact of our new existence? Life! Is there any possibility of missing out on life? No. Are there any exceptions, any exclusion clauses? No. Could it ever be that someone might find themselves unhooked from Christ's belt and joined on to Adam again? Such a thing is absolutely impossible. It is God who has taken us out of Adam, God who has joined us to Christ and, unless he were to change his mind, which he will never do, we are in Christ for ever.

If you are a Christian, you can look at death and see in it a proof of life. As you read the obituary column in your morning paper (and to do this regularly, by the way, is a certain sign of late middle age), every entry tells you that you are joined inevitably to your covenant head. You can walk through a cemetery and look at the gravestones, and every one of them is saying, 'You must share the experience of your covenant head.' But if you are a believer in Christ, this does not make you tremble. Instead, you can say with thankfulness and hope, 'For as in Adam all die, so also in Christ shall all be made alive' (1 Cor. 15:22).

Such is the glorious new relationship into which we have been brought. This is what God has done for us. 'If anyone is in Christ, he is a new creation. The old has passed away; behold, the new has come.' Is it any wonder that Christians sing? What a great thing it is to be in Christ! It does not matter how weak you are, how frail, how fearful. Your future is secure and infinitely wonderful. If you are in Christ, you are safe for ever. But are you in Christ?

The hopeless alternative

It is safe to assume that most of the readers of this book are Christians. But it would be rash to suppose that every reader is. Perhaps you are one of those who are not 'in

Christ' at this point. You have not yet believed in him. You have never repented of your sins, have never turned from them decisively and asked the Lord Jesus to be your Saviour. If this is your situation, can you understand how hopeless your position is? Being a Christian is not a minor matter. It is not a lifestyle choice or an optional extra. It means belonging to a different people, being in an entirely different category as far as God is concerned.

If you are not a Christian, what is the basic fact of your existence, what is your ultimate problem? It is not your character, your personality, the wrong things which you may have done. In a book like this, you may be expecting me to say that your great problem is your sin. But even this is not the fundamental truth about you. The ground-level fact of your being is that you are in Adam. All God's dealings with you are through Adam, and he will only deal with you through Adam as long as you are outside Christ. That means that you can expect from God only death, condemnation, hell and everlasting torment. You are a member of a doomed race, hooked on to Adam's belt.

This being the case, anything you do to try to please God is irrelevant. It does not matter how diligently you attempt to win his favour. You may say, 'I intend to be a better person. I am going to lead a purer thought-life, be more unselfish, more kind and patient. I am going to help other people more. I will stop telling lies. I will read my Bible every day.' None of it will make the slightest difference. You are in Adam! No matter what you do, you cannot satisfy God. The giant is falling and everyone on his belt is falling with him. You may weep and cry out, 'Please be kind to me, God, I am doing my best!' But the giant is doomed and so are you. There is no hope, no way out, there is nothing you can do. There is no alternative to everlasting ruin. Spend, if you like, every moment of your life from now until your death trying to please God. Nothing will make any difference as long as you are in Adam.

On 6 August 1945, a B29 aircraft took off with a strange and terrible cargo. The plane was called the Enola Gay and it was heading for the headquarters of the Second Japanese Imperial Army in a city called Hiroshima. Its cargo was a uranium bomb. The Allied commanders had been advised that if they attempted to invade the mainland of Japan they could lose a million soldiers, with Japanese casualties estimated at between ten and twenty million. Rightly or wrongly—and who of us would have wanted to make the decision?—they decided to try to force the enemy to surrender by demonstrating the power of the weapons at their disposal. This would be done by the destruction of a city of a quarter of a million human beings. Destroy it they did. If you were in Hiroshima that morning, you were doomed. It did not matter what you did. You could have rung up your uncle who had emigrated to America and asked him to call his Congressman. It would have made no difference. You could have put on a pair of blue jeans and a baseball cap and run into the streets waving an American flag. It would not have mattered. You were doomed because Hiroshima was doomed and, whatever you did, you were still in that place.

The position of those trapped in that city is a picture, though imprecise and feeble, of what it means to be in Adam. What a fearful, desolating place to be! For there is a solemn division among human beings, among you who are reading this page. Though not obvious to the eye, it is real and terrible. There are two peoples, two races. Some of you are in Adam and some of you are now in Christ. And the only hope for anyone in the first category is to get out of Adam and into Christ. How can you change over? In yourself you cannot—there is no hope. The only solution—and I pray that you will do this—is to 'believe into Christ'. Cry to the Lord God for mercy. Say to him, 'Lord, I confess that I am a sinner. I was born a sinner, I have an ungodly nature and I know that, if I am not forgiven and changed, I will go to hell. I have learned by now, no matter what I thought before, that I cannot save myself. Dear Lord, take me out of Adam and bring me into Christ. Help me to call on him as my Saviour. Unhook me from Adam's belt and join me to your Son.'

If you ask God to do that for you, he will. He will! He is infinitely gracious and kind. It can happen and it does happen—to thousands every day. Long ago a man realised that he was a lost sinner and he cried out in despair, 'What must I do to be saved?' What must I do to get out of Adam and into Christ? The answer was crystal clear: 'Believe in the Lord Jesus, and you will be saved, you and your household' (Acts 16:30,31). It does not matter who you are or what you have done. It does not matter how wicked you may have been, for God is rich in mercy.

On a cross at Calvary hung an evil man with only a short time to live. Knowing that he was facing everlasting condemnation, he cried to Jesus, on a cross beside him, for mercy. The Lord did not tell him to straighten out his life and try to do better. Nor did he say that it was too late for him. The words of the holy Son of God to this poor wretch were, 'Truly, I say to you, today you will be with me in Paradise' (Luke 23:43). Think of it! A prayer to Christ and, in a moment, his destiny was changed from hell to heaven.

Will you ask the Lord Jesus to save you? Do you realise what it means to be in Adam? Do you understand that God is willing to take you and put you into his Son, with all that this means? It will be more significant than anything else that could ever happen to you in the rest of your life. I pray that God will enable you to do so.

2
We who died to sin

Supposing you were to read the following in a book about holiness: 'The problem with some Christians today is that they are trying too hard. They are too up-tight, too worried about doing their duty, too focused on what sort of people they ought to be and how they ought to behave. They are over-anxious about meeting God's requirements. All they need to do is relax, realise how much he loves them and enjoy the blessings which he has given them in Christ.' Would that seem to you a typically shallow piece of modern 'feel-good' religion? Would you disregard its advice as, at best, frivolous and, at worst, dangerous?

It comes, in fact (in my loose paraphrase, admittedly), from the Puritan theologian John Owen, one of the most profound teachers ever to enrich the Christian church. To quote him exactly,

> Unacquaintedness with . . . our privileges, is our sin as well as our trouble . . . This makes us go heavily, when we might rejoice; and to be weak, where we might be strong in the Lord.[11]

Why do we struggle as Christians? 'Unacquaintedness with our privileges', says Owen. We have not familiarised ourselves with the blessings which are ours in Christ. We simply do not realise the magnitude of all that God has done for us. If we did, we would be different people.

Our subject in this chapter is sin in the life of a believer. For every Christian on earth does sin. None of us lives as we should. And this is not a new problem, because Paul was dealing with it two thousand years ago in the sixth chapter of Romans. Not only do all professed believers sin, but many are not particularly concerned or alarmed about their sin.

In Paul's day, apparently, some went even further by daring to defend their disobedient living and, to make matters worse, to do so by quoting Paul and enlisting him in their support! They seemed to have argued like this: 'You have taught us, Paul, the astounding truth that God justifies the ungodly, that he imputes to the wickedest sinner who believes in Jesus the perfect righteousness of Christ himself. You have explained how we are not saved by anything we can ever do, but only by Christ.' So far, so good. That was exactly what Paul taught and what he wants us to understand and believe with all our hearts. This gospel is also intended to make us think, to draw conclusions, which is what these people were doing. 'What shall we say then?', they asked (Rom. 6:1). Excellent! We should all try to work out the implications of our salvation. We should reflect on how God has saved us in Christ and consider what difference it will make to our lives.

But it was the false conclusion at which they arrived which was so grievous for Paul to hear. 'Are we to continue in sin that grace may abound?' Do you see their perverted logic? 'We are following your advice, Paul, continuing along the line which you have drawn for us. God deals with sin in grace. There is enough grace for every sin. The more sin, the more grace and, therefore, the more glory to God. So the more we sin, the greater will be God's grace to us and the more abundant will be the glory which will come to him. In any case, if we were not saved by righteous living in the first place, why bother with righteous living now, when we have been saved and are united to Christ?'

A modern mindset

Such a view is not just an ancient heresy, but a mindset deeply embedded in much of modern evangelicalism. A favourite Bible verse for many professing Christians today, popular because they think it excuses them in their careless living, is Romans 6:14: 'you are not under law but under grace'. They interpret these words to mean that they are under no obligation to keep the law of God.

I remember seeing a car bumper sticker with the words: 'Christians aren't perfect—just forgiven.' In a sense, of course, that is true. We who are believers know very well that we are far from perfect. We do not profess to be. We are sinners saved by God's grace. But that is not what the sticker was meaning. It was a cute little phrase designed to let Christians off the hook of cross-bearing and costly obedience. It was meant to sweep away at a stroke all the striving after holiness that previous generations knew, all the struggling against sin and all the concern to remain separate from the world. 'We don't need to worry about being holy, for we aren't perfect—just forgiven.'

Tragically, this disregard for godliness has infected wide sectors of the contemporary church. Too many professing Christians are not significantly different in their patterns of behaviour from the society in which they live. They fall into the same sexual sin, let themselves become obese or alcohol-dependent, are just as materialistic and pleasure-loving as those around them. The divorce rate among those who call themselves Christians in the Western world is as high as that of unbelievers. They spend the same amount of time watching television, usually identical programmes. Apart from a morning hour of worship, they treat the Lord's Day much as any other day of the week. Many of them are no kinder, more loving or more trust-worthy than people who make no religious profession at all. A majority rarely spend more than two or three min-utes, at most, in daily prayer. The salt has lost its taste (Matt. 5:13). To the question 'Shall we continue in sin that grace may abound?' they have, subconsciously perhaps, answered 'Of course!'

Paul rejects this answer with horror: 'By no means!' (v.2). Never think of it! Such a conclusion is not to be con-templated for a moment! But on what basis does he reject it? Because of union with Christ. This union makes it inconceivable that we should plan to continue in sin.

To understand this is of the greatest practical importance for every Christian. We are, I hope, concerned about our sins. We may have learned that the 'quick fix' approach does not work, so we are not chasing after some experience or spiritual technique which will lift us swiftly and effortlessly to a higher plane of living, where indwelling sin will no longer affect us. But we are dissatisfied with ourselves and we do long to be more like our Lord Jesus. So how are we to go about it?

Let us follow Paul as he shows the relevance of union with Christ to personal holiness. His answer is summarised in what is one of the most transforming truths of this wonder-ful letter: 'How can we who died to sin still live in it?' (v.2).

Our new identity

What is a Christian? As we saw in the previous chapter, a Christian is a person 'in Christ', someone who has been removed from one covenant representative to another. It is true that we enter Christ by exercising faith. Yet we have learned that ultimately this transfer is brought about by the almighty power of God. It is not a matter first and foremost of our felt experience, some change that we sense inside us, although a profound inner revolution has most certainly taken place. Instead, it has reference to our standing, our status, our position.

We are associated with a different Head. We have become members of a different people. We have moved from one dominion to another, as Paul teaches when he writes that God 'has delivered us from the domain of darkness and transferred us to the kingdom of his beloved Son' (Col. 1:13). He is now dealing with us on an entirely new basis, always through Jesus Christ. We are living a new existence in a new realm, a new world. 'If anyone is in Christ, he is a new creation. The old has passed away; behold, the new has come' (2 Cor. 5:17).

In other words, as Christians we have a radically new identity, so different that the Bible describes it as being born all over again (John 1:13), and it is this new identity which is the foundation for our holiness. Why are we to become like Christ? Because we are already in him. The Scripture underlines this by telling us that we have already been set apart by God, that we are already sanctified.

Such terminology may sound strange to us, for we are more familiar with the idea of sanctification as a process, a work which continues over a long period. So it is. By the working of the Holy Spirit we are 'enabled more and more to die unto sin, and live unto righteousness'.[12] Day after day, year after year, we 'put to death the deeds of the body' (Rom. 8:13) and are transformed progressively into the image of Christ. But the New Testament can also speak of sanctification as a momentary, once-for-all transaction—what theologians sometimes call 'definitive sanctification'—when God separates us to himself by taking us out of Adam and placing us in Christ.

Paul, for example, when writing to the church in Corinth, described the believers as 'those sanctified in Christ Jesus' (1 Cor. 1:2). Now this was a very imperfect church. Some of its members were petty-minded, their thinking was confused, several had become entangled in immorality. The public witness of the fellowship was marred by divisions and worldliness. So how can Paul call them 'sanctified'? He means that they have been given, once and for all, a new identity—since they are no longer in Adam, but now in Christ.

'We who died to sin'

How is the new identity described? 'We who died to sin' (Rom. 6:2). This is a more accurate translation than 'we died to sin', as, for example, in the New International Version. The Greek of the original text has the sense: 'we whose characteristic, whose distinguishing mark, whose peculiar identity it is that we died to sin'. This is who we are, this is what marks us out. A Christian is a 'died-to-sin' man or woman. Paul goes on to amplify this in verses 3-10, as he deals with our union with Christ in his death and resurrection.

For Christ 'died to sin, once for all' (Rom. 6:10). In other words, his connection with sin was broken for ever. It was not that sin had any foothold in his heart, that he was personally guilty of sin or involved in it in that way. He was 'holy, innocent, unstained, separated from sinners' (Heb. 7:26). But he came to earth and lived in a sinful world and, as John Murray puts it, 'sin may be said to have ruled over him in that his humiliation state was conditioned by the sin with which he was vicariously identified'.[13]

Never could Jesus escape the sights and sounds of sin. Greek cities—and there were several within walking distance of his home in Nazareth—were full of the depravity with which we are sadly familiar in our own society. Human nature was as wicked then as it is now. He was acquainted with drunkards and thieves, misers and liars, prostitutes and crooks. Examples of injustice, cruelty and selfishness presented themselves to him daily. He himself was tempted ferociously, 'in every respect . . . as we are' (Heb. 4:15). He suffered ill-treatment, was hated, felt the pain of cutting slander. We cannot suppose, for example, that the pregnancy of his unmarried mother remained a secret in small-town Galilee, which explains the poisoned sneer of his enemies, 'We were not born of sexual immorality' (John 8:41).

What must it have meant for a perfectly holy being to live in that environment? If worldly, compromising Lot was 'greatly distressed by the sensual conduct of the wicked (. . . tormenting his righteous soul over their lawless deeds that he saw and heard)' (2 Pet. 2:7,8), how excruciatingly painful must it have been for a mind and soul of unsullied purity to be in intimate contact with so much that was corrupt! For over thirty years he lived in the nauseating atmosphere of sin, at a cost to himself which we cannot begin to imagine.

Then he died and, as definitive evidence of his death, was buried. He thus broke with the world of sin for ever. 'He died to sin, once for all.' He will never return to that world. Never again will he be tempted by sin, never suffer further from its renewed assaults. Our representative died to sin and left it behind, and his death 'meant the end of

Christ's being in the realm of sin'.[14] The giant, on whose belt we now hang, is in a new sphere where sin can no longer have any impact upon him.

What then does that imply for those of us who are in Christ? It means that, because we are joined to him, we too have died to this world of sin. Our connection with it has been broken finally and for all time. We have been taken out of Adam and we are never going to return. Not only did the Lord Jesus Christ die for us, but we died in him. Paul emphasises that truth strongly in this passage, making the point no fewer than six times in seven verses:

> we who died to sin . . . all of us who have been baptized into Christ Jesus were baptized into his death . . . We were buried therefore with him by baptism into death . . . we have been united with him in a death like his . . . our old self was crucified with him . . . we have died with Christ.
> (Romans 6:2,3,4,5,6,8)

Such is our identity. We died. Paul does not say that we ought to have died or that we want to die, or should try to die, or one day will die. No! 'We have died with Christ.' We cannot continue in the old relationship with the world of sin, because we died to it. Someone who has died cannot continue a relationship with those who are left, for death means the ending of all such connections. Why do we grieve for loved ones taken from us? Because in this life we will never make contact with them again.

Not only did the Lord Jesus die, but he was raised to a glorious new existence and lives now in a new dimension. As Paul puts it, 'the life he lives he lives to God' (v.10). And that also is true of us. For we too, having died to sin, have been raised to life in a new world, and this life we live in God's strength and for his glory. Our identification with Christ in his death is not an end in itself, but so that 'just as Christ was raised from the dead by the glory of the Father, we too might walk in newness of life' (v.4). This is the magnitude of what has happened to us; this is its awesome reality. Salvation is the determinative, ultimate, supernatural transfer.

So many people have never understood the overwhelming hugeness of conversion. It means leaving the old world of sin and entering the new world of living in, with and for God. This is who we are as Christians. And it is this transfer which makes the original question sound so foolish: 'Are we to continue in sin?' Continue in sin? Keep on living in that old world from which we were rescued? Yielding to its impulses, craving its pleasures, living for its rewards? What a ludicrous idea! To be a Christian is, by definition, to have been removed from the realm of sin. How can we continue in the realm from which we have been everlastingly delivered? Our new identity makes this a nonsense question. 'How can we who died to sin still live in it?'

Imagine a Christian businessman who is often away from home, travelling all over the world, staying in various hotels in the great cities. One day a colleague says to him, 'When you are away on these trips, there is nothing to prevent you from being unfaithful to your wife, is there? She doesn't know where you go, whom you meet or how you spend your time. No one does. She hasn't hired a private detective to follow you. There are no constraints of any kind on what you choose to do. Why do you not cheat on her? You could get away with it.'

How would he answer? Surely it would be with mingled anger and pity. 'My wife means more to me than anyone else ever can or will. She is bone of my bone and flesh of my flesh. I love her more than my life. Do you think that there is anything on earth that would induce me to betray her or hurt her? The very fact that you ask the question tells me that you know nothing about what being a husband means. You simply do not understand what a real marriage is. In fact, you know nothing about love. I'm sorry for you.'

If you are seriously thinking about continuing in sin as a believer, or if your life is characterised by disobedience to God, then I must ask you, 'Are you a Christian at all?' We saw in the previous chapter that human beings can be divided into two groups, and two only: those in Adam and those in Christ. But there is a sub-group: those who think they are in Christ, but are still in Adam. Many people profess to be Christians, some even describing themselves as 'born again'. They mean it sincerely and would be annoyed if anyone were to question it. But they show no evidence of being changed. There is no real sign that they have been transferred into a different world, given a radically new identity. You cannot honestly conclude that they appear to be among those who have been taken out of Adam and brought into Christ.

Can you say truthfully that this is your new identity? That you are a dead-to-sin person? Have you been changed? Are you a new man, a new woman? Are you living in a new world? The reason why so many today are looking for a second spiritual experience is that they have never had a true first experience. They think that they need something to liven them up as Christians, when they may never have received new life in the first place. They have never been converted, never made new creatures. The Christian is someone with a new identity.

Our new responsibility

'But', you may feel like saying, 'it is all very well to tell us that we have died to sin, that we have been brought out of Adam and into Christ, but what about the brute fact of our wrongdoing, our disobedience? I am painfully aware that sin is a reality in my own experience. How can I act more consistently on the basis of my new identity? How can I overcome temptation? How can I live a life which is holy? What help can you provide for me?'

So, in verses 11-14, Paul turns to the practical aspect and gives us three exhortations. If I devote more time to the first than to the two which follow, it is not because they are less important, but because the emphasis of the first exhortation is often neglected.

Reckon

'You . . . must consider yourselves dead to sin and alive to God in Christ Jesus' (verse 11).

Our great need in all of this is to realise our true position, for 'the major secret of holy living is in the mind'.[15] So, throughout this passage, Paul constantly emphasises the importance of knowing, of understanding: 'Do you not know? . . . We know . . . We know . . .' (vv.3,6,9). We need to know.

People today have no time for biblical doctrine. They call it impractical and useless. But doctrine is the most practical thing in the world. 'You will know the truth', said Jesus, 'and the truth will set you free' (John 8:32). If we are to live as we should, we need to be instructed in what union with Christ means and to understand it. 'Above all,' says Paul, 'you need to practise thinking of yourselves in this way.' 'Consider yourselves dead to sin.' We could translate this as: 'keep on reckoning yourselves dead to sin and alive to God'. Make this your practice, your habit. Never allow yourself to forget who you are. Moment by moment, day by day, year by year, drum into your consciousness that this is your true new identity.

It is a striking fact that this is the first exhortation in the letter to the Romans, the first time that we are told to do anything. Is that not remarkable? Five and a half chapters pass before we are given a single command! Paul has shown us at length our need of salvation, he has declared God's provision in Christ, he has spoken of the peace and assurance which that brings to the believer and has explained what union with Christ means. Before he tells us to do anything—in other words, before pointing us to our duty—he fills our minds and hearts with what God has done for us in his Son.

The very structure of this letter therefore is a call to us first of all to sit down, be quiet and listen! Listen to God, understand what he is saying, believe it and worship. In ordinary grammar, the indicative mood is used for statements, the imperative mood for commands. So we can say that, in the grammar of the gospel, the indicatives precede and make possible the imperatives. James Philip comments on verses 12 and 13 that

> these imperatives are based on the indicatives in 1-10, and they are possible of fulfilment because the indicatives are true and supply both the inspiration and the dynamic for such ethical endeavour.[16]

This is what John Owen meant when he stated that the main reason for our spiritual heaviness and weakness is 'unacquaintedness with our privileges'. He was certainly not decrying effort in the Christian life. No one could read

much of Owen and think such a thing. He dealt exten-
sively with such topics as 'Mortification of sin',
'Temptation' and 'Indwelling sin in believers'. 'Be killing
sin or it will be killing you', he wrote.[17] He laid enormous
stress on the importance of a diligent, costly, lifelong
struggle with personal sin. But the great point is that he
always puts our earnest, persevering efforts into the context of grace and faith. What God has done provides the
basis for what we must do.

A tightrope

For the life of godliness is a tightrope, with danger on
either side. On one side is carelessness, disobedience,
worldliness—a shoddy, second-rate version of Christianity.
We have referred already to frivolous, self-proclaimed 'born-
again believers' who show little regard for God's law, God's
day, God's will. We see that error and want to escape it. But
we can forget the danger on the other side and, in trying to
avoid one mistake, topple over into the opposite extreme.
This is the deadly error of legalism. It was the error of the
Pharisees. They were originally pious people, intensely sin-
cere. They were willing to die for God's truth, and many of
them did. But, as time passed, they lost grace and everything
turned into law and duty so that, instead of being humble
and thankful, they became self-confident and proud.

Paul wrote to young Christians who were in danger of
falling off the tightrope: 'O foolish Galatians! . . . Having
begun by the Spirit, are you now being perfected by the
flesh?' (Gal. 3:1,3). They were trying to be 'perfected by
the flesh'. It can happen easily. Are you or I in danger of
becoming legalists? Are too many sermons couched in the
language of 'Do . . . do . . . do'? How many of us approach
our Christian life with what my teacher wanted me to hear

when she used to write on my school report, 'Must try harder'? Do you find yourself thinking that what you need above all is to do more for God? More prayer, more Bible-reading, more study, more commitment, more evangelism?

Please do not misunderstand me. Many of us should be doing more of these things. We do need to try harder. We ought to be serving Christ with every atom of our beings. But all too often the focus is wrong. We begin and end with ourselves, we turn salvation into a human activity, we forget about God's grace and his invincible purpose to bless. It all becomes a matter of dull determination, wrestling all the while against an increasing sense of hopelessness and frustration.

But such an approach simply does not work! I had to learn that at the beginning of my ministry. I found that, with the best of intentions, I was scolding my people, wounding their consciences by outlining their shortcomings, urging them to do better, to try harder. Some of them would try, would improve for a short time—but then, almost always, fall back again into the old patterns. Instead of helping them, I was making them anxious, burdened, weighed down with a sense of yet more failure. They were coming to think of God as the man in the parable thought of his master: 'I knew you to be a hard man' (Matt. 25:24).

But he is not a hard God! He is merciful, compassionate and tender. He does not frown at our pathetic efforts at obeying him, tut-tutting and telling us how disappointed he is. Instead he is like a father watching his young child trying to form her first letters and saying with delight, 'That's great, sweetheart! Some day you'll be able to write even better than that.'

I remember talking with a Christian lady who told me that she dreaded coming to the Lord's Table because, by the time her pastor had finished his sermons on the need for self-examination and how unworthy we all are, she wanted to crawl into a hole and hide. What a travesty of the gospel! Its message is not 'Do, do' but 'Believe and receive.' It is good news of Christ and his salvation freely given to all who will come to him. Our great problem is not lack of effort, but 'unacquaintedness with our privileges'.

Try harder?

I play golf. I am using, you understand, the terms 'play' and 'golf' loosely, but, however unspeakably bad the result, I do enjoy the game and at least no one can fault me for lack of effort. Some golfers are a disgrace to the game, for in my view they do not try hard enough. They draw back the club effortlessly, bring it down effortlessly, strike the ball effortlessly and see it soar down the middle of the fairway. Not me! I grit my teeth, take a deep breath, grip the club tightly with veins bulging, and come down on the ball with every ounce of beef and muscle. (I can't understand why it rarely travels far, and never in a straight line.) They walk off the course, having played eighteen holes in a mere seventy-five or eighty strokes. I can say with perfect honesty that I have never finished a round without striking the ball well over one hundred times! I work so much harder than they do. Plenty of effort! So why am I so discouragingly incompetent? Because I was never taught to play the game. I simply do not have the resources or knowledge necessary. My efforts are misdirected, entrenching bad habits instead of correcting them. The harder I try, the worse I become, because I really have no idea what I am supposed to be doing.

I wonder how many people are trying to live the Christian life in the same way as I play golf? 'Try harder' is their credo. But their focus is wrong. The context of our Christian living is not 'I must'. Instead, it is 'He has'. And to start from God and what he has done for us will make all the difference. Walter Marshall, in *The Gospel Mystery of Sanctification*, written in 1692, explains how 'We must first receive the comforts of the Gospel, that we may be able to perform . . . the duties of the law.'[18] This is the true balance. He is not against law, not commending careless-ness or lack of effort. We ought to 'perform the duties of the law'—of that there can be no question. But how? By first 'receiving the comforts of the Gospel'.

Sometimes we hear Christ spoken of as our example. In a sense that is true. He is an example to us, the best and most inspiring possible. 'For I have given you an example,' he said, after washing the feet of his disciples, 'that you also should do just as I have done to you' (John 13:15). Peter exhorts his readers to suffer injustice patiently, 'because Christ also suffered for you, leaving you an example, so that you might follow in his steps' (1 Pet. 2:21). We can do no better than keep the example of his life and character constantly before us and try our utmost to imitate him.

But what if our Lord were nothing more than a perfect example? For an example, instead of helping, can disable and discourage. Think of the boy whose father is a natural athlete, gifted at every sport, while his son is poorly co-ordinated and clumsy. His father takes the football or cricket bat and says, 'Look, son, here is how to do it. It's quite easy!' But every time his father shows him, the boy shrinks further into himself, because he just cannot do it. What good is an example, if we do not have the ability to follow it? Or imagine the girl whose older sister was aca-demically brilliant at school, top of the class in every sub-ject. But the teachers now hold her up as an example to her less gifted sister, and the example becomes a horrible burden, crushing her down.

What good would it be to us if Jesus Christ were nothing more than an example? It would torture us by setting before us a standard of perfection which we would be bound to try to imitate but could never attain. Yet how many people are trying to follow the example of Christ in their own strength? Is it any surprise that they fail? As James S. Stewart puts it,

> The evangel of an ethical example is a devastating thing. It makes religion the most grievous of burdens. Perhaps this is the real reason why, even among professing Christians, there are so many strained faces and weary hearts and captive, unreleased spirits. They have listened to Jesus' teaching, they have meditated on Jesus' character; and then they have risen up, and tried to drive their own lives along Jesus' royal way. Disappointment heaped on bitter disappointment has been the result. The great example has been a deadweight beating them down, bearing them to the ground, bowing their hopeless souls in the dust.[19]

No, the Lord Jesus is, thank God, far more than an example. He is the Saviour. He is our mighty covenant Head, in whom we have a glorious new existence. And the secret to living this new life is to realise that we have it, to believe that it is ours. We tend to undervalue faith by thinking of it as something ethereal, insubstantial. 'We know all about faith,' we say, 'but give us something practical, some concrete advice on how to be holy. Show us something real and solid, a plan that we can follow, something that we can do.'

But faith is more powerful and effective than anything else. 'Consider yourselves dead to sin and alive to God', says Paul. There is nothing more practical than this. Acquaint yourselves with your privileges; soak yourselves in the reality of your identity in Christ, who you now are by God's grace. Meditate on this. Take time over it. Pray it in, praise it in, reflect on it, absorb yourselves in it constantly. When you get up in the morning, when you are leaving home for work, when you sit down to relax in the evening, say to yourself, 'I am dead to sin and alive to God in Christ.' In everything you do and say, think about yourself like this.

Sanctification is simply becoming who we are. 'Don't be a baby', we hear people saying. But to whom do they say it? Not to an infant—he or she is a baby and can be nothing else. It would be pointless and cruel to speak to them in this way. But you could say it to a teenager, to a twenty-year-old. 'Don't be a baby!' Why? Because they are not babies. Or, to change the illustration,

> To say to the slave who has not been emancipated, 'Do not behave as a slave', is to mock his enslavement. But to say the same to the slave who has been set free is the necessary appeal to put into effect the privileges and rights of his liberation.[20]

In other words, 'Be who you are.' So the call to the believer is, 'Do not be dominated by sin.' Why? Because that is who you are—in Christ, free from sin's dominion. Stewart writes that

> a Christian is a man who strives, every day he lives, to make more and more real and actual and visible and

52

convincing that which he is ideally and potentially by his union with Jesus Christ . . . His relationship to Christ constrains him. It is a fact, but it is also a duty. It is a present reality, but also a beckoning ideal.[21]

Live out your new identity!

God's people do not so much need the whip of rebuke as the encouragement of an increasing awareness of what God has done for us, how gloriously he has changed us. John Owen reminds us that 'a due sense of deliverance from the dominion of sin is the most effectual motive unto . . . holiness'.[22] To know that we are new people is the best starting point for living as new people.

The story is told of Augustine, who had been an immoral man before his conversion, that, after he became a Christian, he met a woman with whom he had once had a sinful relationship. Coming up to him with a suggestive smile, she taunted him with, 'It is I, Augustine.' 'Yes,' he said, 'but it is not I, Augustine.' 'You . . . must consider yourselves dead to sin and alive to God in Christ Jesus.'

Yet Paul has more to tell us.

Refuse

'Let not sin therefore reign in your mortal bodies, to make you obey their passions' (verse 12).

Refuse to serve your old master! For sin is represented as a master in this passage. It desires to 'reign' (v.12), to have 'dominion' over us (v.14), to direct us as once it did. It is a malignant, alien power, seeking to re-establish over us its lost control, and it can use our 'mortal bodies' as a bridge-head through which to govern us. And Paul is ordering us not to listen to that old master, not to obey sin or allow it to influence us in any way. 'Do not let the devil deceive you', says the apostle. 'Do not let him get away with the pretence that he still rules you. Reject that destructive authority from which you have been delivered.' 'Let not sin therefore reign in your mortal bodies, to make you obey their passions. Do not present your members to sin as instruments for unrighteousness' (vv.12,13).

Here is the negative of holiness—the sharp, painful 'No!' to temptation. We must say that 'No!' for ourselves, for God will not say it for us. He will not make us holy apart from our own conscious efforts. The new life is not automatically ours. We are to pursue it actively. Refusing to sin is essential—a simple response, in a way, but one which demands unwearying perseverance. This is where the effort comes in—after grace and empowered by grace —but indispensable nonetheless. Christ within us enables us to keep on saying no to sin. Should it mean the tearing out of an eye or the cutting off of a hand (Matt. 5:29,30), we say no to sin. It has no longer any claim on us.

Whenever we give in to temptation, the fault is entirely ours. James Fraser writes of believers who fall, 'If sin shall now reign and prevail, it must be owing to their own indolence, unwatchfulness, faulty weakness or treachery. Sin hath not now force enough to restore and maintain its own dominion.'[23] Satan cannot compel us to sin, and we are to refuse his commands and turn away from his seduction.

To return to the illustration of the emancipated slave, we might think back to the first day of January 1863 when Abraham Lincoln, the American president, issued a proclamation stating that

all persons held as slaves within any State or designated part of a State, the people whereof shall be in rebellion against the United States, shall be then, thenceforward, and for forever free; and the Executive Government of the United States, including the military and naval authority thereof, will recognize and maintain the freedom of such persons.

Imagine a black man who has escaped from one of the Southern states, travelled north and thus become a free man, a slave no longer. But one day, as he walks along the street, he sees his old master, who raises his hand and says, 'Come here, boy.' For a moment, conditioned as he is by years of obedience, the ex-slave starts out towards the person who has commanded him for so long. But then he remembers Lincoln's proclamation, stops and says to himself, 'Wait a moment. He isn't my master any more. I don't have to listen to anything he says.' And he turns his back on the man who once had owned him and walks away.

Is that not exactly what the devil tries to do with us? 'Come here', he says. We have obeyed him for so long and there is still something within us that wants to obey, so that, without considering, without reflecting, we start obeying him again. 'Refuse to do that', says Paul. 'Remember that you are now free.' 'Let not sin therefore reign in your mortal bodies, to make you obey . . . Do not present your members to sin as instruments for unrighteousness' (vv.12,13a).

The next time you are tempted to sin, remember who you are and refuse to listen. When Satan comes to you, challenge him: 'Who do you think I am? What sort of person? You hold out to me these sickening, contemptible sins. Do you think that I am going to give in to them now that I am in Christ? Never!'

But we are not to be satisfied with a purely negative response.

Rededicate

'Present yourselves to God as those who have been brought from death to life, and your members to God as instruments for righteousness' (verse 13b).

Positively, this is what we must do. The verb translated 'present' often refers to offering a sacrifice. We find the same word later in this epistle when believers are called to 'present your bodies as a living sacrifice' (Rom. 12:1). So the meaning here would be that we are to place ourselves and all that we are upon the altar in glad surrender to God. Or it can mean 'to put at someone's disposal', as when a Roman tribune told his centurions to '*provide* mounts for Paul to ride' (Acts 23:24). In either case, the meaning is clear. We have to offer ourselves to God. We are to give to our Master our thoughts, our imaginations, our hearts, our eyes, our tongues, our hands, our feet. 'Lord Jesus,' we are to say, 'here I am, yours to command. You have brought me from miserable death to abundant life and I am giving myself to the high privilege of serving you, to be what you want me to be, go where you want me to go, say what you want me to say, do what you want me to do.' We are to spend our hours and our years doing all we can to please and serve God.

Isaac Watts wrote, in one of his songs for children,

> *In works of labour or of skill*
> *I would be busy too:*
> *For Satan finds some mischief still*
> *For idle hands to do.*

It is quite true. The best way to overcome sin is to be busy in our Master's service. We will not make progress by sitting and endlessly examining our souls in morbid introspection. Nor by becoming hypochondriacs, wrapped up in ourselves, constantly taking our spiritual temperature. Our call is to do our duty in the world, for the church on earth is, after all, the church militant.

> What we all need is not a doctor, but a sergeant major. Here we are, as it were, slouching about the parade ground, feeling our own pulses, feeling miserable, talking about our weakness . . . You have no business to be slouching about like that; stand on your feet, realize who and what you are, enlisted in the army of God.[24]

There is a place for heart-searching and self-examination. But it must be allied with a brave, diligent energy in the work of the kingdom. When we are so engaged, we are no longer so vulnerable to the devil. As J. I. Packer puts it, 'The Christian's motto should not be "Let go and let God" but "Trust God and get going!"'[25]

And the passage ends with a liberating promise: 'For sin will have no dominion over you, since you are not under law but under grace' (v.14). This does not mean that God's law has been abolished and so we can sin without it mattering. Not at all! 'You are not under law but under grace' is just another way of saying that we are not in Adam but in Christ. As believers, we are no longer dominated by a condemning, destructive law. We are in the grace of Christ and sin therefore cannot have dominion over us. For we are in the body of Christ and all his life and power and strength and enabling are available for us.

Well could Dr Lloyd-Jones write of Romans 6, 'Personally, I found my new understanding of it to be one of the most liberating experiences in my Christian life.'[26] We are no longer in Adam, but in Christ, and we are called to realise this and live in light of it. In the words of James S. Stewart,

> 'Christ in me' means Christ bearing me along from within . . . Christ giving my whole life a wonderful poise and lift, and turning every burden into wings . . . it is release and liberty, life with an endless song at its heart. It means feeling within you, as long as life here lasts, the carrying power of Love Almighty; and underneath you, when you come to die, the touch of everlasting arms.[27]

We are not under law, but we are—thank God!—under grace. What a wonderful salvation!

3
Abide in me

'Let not your hearts be troubled', said Jesus to his disciples (John 14:1). He could see fear etched on their faces and hear quavers of anxiety in their voices as they talked together. Why were they so disturbed? Because their Master was leaving them. He had already told them more than once that he was going to die, but they had been reluctant to take him seriously. Now, however, the message was unmistakably clear: 'Little children, yet a little while I am with you . . . Where I am going you cannot come' (John 13:33). And they were horrified.

How would they manage in his absence? For three years he had been a constant presence in their lives. They had watched him, listened to him, learned so much from his example and teaching. His love had touched them, his purity had challenged them, and they had been awed and excited by his miracles. He had strengthened them when they were weak and guided them in times of uncertainty. How could they cope when he was with them no longer?

'Because I have said these things to you, sorrow has filled your heart' (John 16:6), Christ said. For he knew, and wanted them to realise that he knew, exactly how they were feeling. And so, in chapters 14–17 of John's Gospel, in what is often called 'The Farewell Discourse', we find the Lord encouraging them: 'I will come again and will take you to myself . . . I will not leave you as orphans; I will come to you . . . it is to your advantage that I go away' (John 14:3,18;16:7).

This is the context, often overlooked, of chapter 15, with its command, 'Abide in me' (v.4). No words could have been better calculated to hearten these apprehensive men. For what Christ is telling them is that, in the truest sense, he is not leaving them. So intimately and unbreakably are they united with him that nothing, not even death, can separate them. Through the ministry of his representative, the Holy Spirit, they will continue to experience the blessings of his presence.

And it is this experience to which we now turn. For being in Christ is more than having a new legal status in God's sight. It is richer than 'considering' our new identity, grasping it by faith and acting upon that basis. We are meant to sense it, to luxuriate in it, to realise within ourselves, in every aspect of our beings, that we are actually 'in him'—what the old theologians called 'union *and communion*'. In John Murray's words,

> The life of true faith cannot be that of cold metallic consent. It must have the passion and warmth of love and communion, because communion with God is the crown and apex of true religion.[28]

This intimacy, this personal knowing and enjoying, is expressed in the Lord's words 'Abide in me'.

The reality which Christ describes

Palestine was a land of vineyards. Outside almost every home was a vine, trained up over a wooden structure to provide a shady place where the family could sit and talk together over a meal. Nothing would have been more familiar to the people of the land than this plant, with its branches, leaves and fruit. So Jesus' call to 'abide' was based on an illustration familiar to every child: 'I am the vine; you are the branches' (v.5). His main point was obvious, for it was clear that all life and vigour came from the parent plant. The branch was not fruitful in and of itself. It could never be. On its own it would have been nothing more than a dry, useless stick, fit only for burning. Everything vital and productive, every plump, purple grape, was received from the vine.

The same is true of us in the spiritual sphere. Our fruitfulness depends entirely on our being joined to the Lord Jesus. We cannot grow or develop from our own resources, but must draw life and strength directly from him. This means that union with Christ is not merely a legal connection or abstract idea, but a living, intensely dynamic personal relationship. It involves a continual outflow of spiritual energy from him to us.

We cannot by our own efforts make ourselves into the people God intends us to be. We cannot change ourselves in any profound or lasting way. But Christ can—and does. He transforms us. He enables us to overcome sin and grow in grace. He equips us to do his will and uses us to carry out his purposes in the world. In Paul's words, 'we are his [God's] workmanship, created *in Christ Jesus* for good works' (Eph. 2:10).

There is, as we have seen, an important place for effort in the Christian life. To follow Christ is a path of strenuous endeavour, for we are commanded to 'work out your own salvation with fear and trembling'. But, as Paul immediately adds, 'it is God who works in you, both to will and to work for his good pleasure' (Phil. 2:12-13). Here is the vine, invigorating the branches.

Holiness does not come about by a determined process of self-reformation. Many earnest people have tried that, and all have failed. Martin Luther is a supreme example. He often fasted, sometimes for three days at a stretch. He subjected his body to extremes of exhaustion and cold to see if this would help make him more godly. He confessed his sins to a priest every day, on one occasion for six hours without a break. 'If I had kept on any longer,' he testifies, 'I should have killed myself with vigils, prayers, reading and other work.' His energy and devotion achieved nothing, and he had to learn, through believing the gospel of God's free grace in his Son, that growth and productiveness are the direct result of the living Christ at work in our lives. As D. A. Carson puts it, 'the union between Christ and his followers . . . stands at the heart of spiritual vitality'.[29]

The activity of the risen Lord

This is vividly illustrated in the book of Acts. Its fuller title, 'The Acts of the Apostles', is in a sense a misnomer, for Luke introduces the book by reminding Theophilus of how, in his earlier Gospel, 'I have dealt with all that *Jesus* began to do and teach' (Acts 1:1). He is implying that this second volume will be an account of all that Jesus continued to do and teach after his ascension into heaven. The ministry of the apostles, especially that of Peter and Paul, is certainly described, but again and again the emphasis is on the activity of the risen Lord through them.

Peter and others of the Twelve preached and the church grew, but it was because '*the Lord* added to their number day by day those who were being saved' (2:47). In Philippi, Lydia listened to Paul's message to the women at the riverside, but she became a Christian only when '*the*

Lord opened her heart' (16:14). After Peter and John had been used to heal a lame beggar at the Temple gate, Peter was categorical in explaining how the miracle had happened:

> Men of Israel, why do you wonder at this, or why do you stare at us, as though by our own power or piety we have made him walk? . . . the faith that is *through Jesus* has given the man this perfect health in the presence of you all.
>
> (3:12,16)

When something unusual happened, the early church made a point of saying to the watching world, 'It is Jesus who is doing this.'

This makes sense in light of what we have learned already. We are 'in Christ', hooked to his belt, in Thomas Goodwin's illustration, and it is his activity which is ultimately crucial. He is the one who counts! It is good for us to remember this in a man-centred age in which the predominant stress, even in the church, is on our vision, our ideas, what we intend to do. Religious publicity machines focus attention on the 'personality' and achievements of popular leaders. All too often the impression is given that humans are driving and controlling the work of the kingdom. But what really matters is what Christ plans to accomplish and the fact that we are united to him. He is the source of all life and fruitfulness. When we see branches loaded with grapes, we know—or should know—that they come not from the branches but the vine.

And what is utterly thrilling is that he does choose to work through us. Now that our Lord is in heaven, he no longer extends his kingdom in person. Instead, we have the privilege of being the medium through which the living, reigning

Christ exerts his power and grace in the world. We are his body on earth, the instruments through whom he redeems his people and restores his sin-scarred creation. The task entrusted to us is massive, the reality behind it awesome.

The reassurance which Christ offers

'Abide in me.' Think of it! 'Remain close to me, joined to me, drawing on my strength, living in my presence.' What a wonderful prospect! But is it not at the same time a little intimidating? The Lord Jesus is, after all, God himself, awesome, terrifying even, in his majesty, holiness and might. Is the thought of 'abiding' in such a being not somewhat daunting? Will such intimate contact with deity not prove to be a demanding, stressful experience? How could we ever relax, even for a moment? Surely the awareness of all our weaknesses and limitations will make us feel tense, constantly under pressure! Being always 'in Christ' might seem like having some immensely important person as a house guest—an honour, but what a strain! 'The responsibility to remain in Jesus . . . can sound so severe, so humourless, so stark, as to evoke fearful and even frenzied compliance, but not love and not joy.'[30] It is a privilege, no doubt, but is it not a rather overwhelming one?

Christ banishes such apprehension by his parallel command, 'Abide in my love', fortified by the reassurance, 'I have loved you' (v.9). He loves us—that is a familiar truth. But do we really appreciate it? How many people do you know who can look you in the eye, tell you 'I love you' and mean it? We are moved when someone says this to us. It is an unforgettable experience, precious, not to be forgotten or taken for granted. And that is the essential and over-riding stance of the Lord Jesus Christ towards each one of his people. To 'abide in me' (v.4) and to 'abide in my love' (v.9) are one and the same thing, for he *is* love as far as we are concerned.

'I have loved you', he said to these disciples. Indeed he had. He had loved them in eternity, when he offered himself as their covenant head. He had loved them in his coming into the world to experience all the limitations and sufferings of earthly life on their behalf. He was about to lay down his life because he loved them. They had been slow to learn, still had many faults, were limited in their abilities—but he loved them. And he has loved you and me in countless ways. Eternity itself will not exhaust the telling of his tenderness and affection towards us.

As . . . so

In explaining how much he loves his disciples he makes a comparison: 'As the Father has loved me, so have I loved you' (v.9). What a staggering statement! Think of God the Father's love for his only-begotten Son—how intense, how all-embracing, how limitless it is! From all eternity he delighted in him. Throughout Christ's earthly life, his Father was upholding him and reassuring him. At crucial moments, as when he was baptised in the Jordan, for example, his voice would ring out, 'You are my beloved Son; with you I am well pleased' (Mark 1:11). And this is how Christ feels towards his people. Nothing else in the universe can serve as a comparison. The parallel is daring, almost shocking, yet unquestionably appropriate from the lips of the One who is Truth itself.

Do we realise as we should the extent of Christ's love for us—its depth, length, breadth and height? Does this fill us with gratitude, move us to delighted worship? Does it mean everything to us? 'See how he loved him!' said the

Jews when they beheld the Lord weeping at the grave of Lazarus (John 11:36). Perhaps that too is the verdict of angels in heaven as they watch and wonder at his dealings with his people, with you and with me.

A question

Yet we may still have a question. 'Abide in my love', says the Lord. But does that mean that his love for us is in doubt in some way, that we might find ourselves outside it, beyond its reach? Surely it is the case that Christ loves his people with a love that never changes and never fails! Is it possible to be loved by him one day but not the next? Does he not love us in spite of who and what we are? Does this command mean that the loss of his love is something we should dread and seek to avoid? Is this why we are told to 'abide'?

It is certainly true that never, to all eternity, will Jesus Christ withdraw his love from a single one of his people. 'Having loved his own who were in the world, he loved them to the end', writes John (13:1), and that love remains as persevering and unconquerable today as ever it was. What, then, does the command to 'abide in my love' mean?

Perhaps we can compare his love with the warmth of the sun. 'The sun is shining today', we say, when the weather is fine. But the sun always shines—uninterruptedly, unbrokenly. We need only soar above the clouds in a plane, even on the dullest day, to see it. Yet at ground level we do not always feel its warmth, for it can be hidden from us by clouds. Although it is still shining, the day is dark and we are cold because the light and heat of the sun are no longer available to us.

So it is with the love of Christ. It shines always upon his people. But it is all too possible for us to deprive ourselves of the awareness of its presence and to live in chilly gloom. The clouds of our sin and neglect come between us and the Saviour and hide from us the warmth of his affection. To 'abide' in his love is to stay in the sunlight, to allow no clouds to come between us. We thus remain in the place where his love for us is a conscious, invigorating reality.

What a reassuring prospect this command holds before us! 'Abide in my love'—knowing it, warming ourselves in it, rejoicing in it, not momentarily but all the time. In Calvin's words, 'He wants us continually to enjoy the love with which He once embraced us and accordingly warns us to beware not to deprive ourselves of it.'[31] Who would not desire such an experience! And it is not a dream, but a reality which Christ wants us to enjoy more and more. But how?

The responsibility which Christ imposes

Our key responsibility is driven home in this verb 'abide', occurring ten times in the first eleven verses of John 15. It means 'to remain, stay, dwell' and implies that a person does not leave a certain place or sphere. Christ defines the sphere of our abiding as himself: 'Abide in me' (vv.4,5,6,7). This abiding is a duty. It is not something which 'just happens'. It does not come about through a mystical experience, nor is it the automatic result of some clever spiritual technique. The verb is an imperative, a command. Here is something we are to do ourselves. We are to give attention to it, to make every effort towards accomplishing it. What is needed is that we should cultivate actively our union with Christ, realising it, experiencing it, so that it becomes the centre around which our life revolves. The responsibility is ours. How then are we to carry it out?

We abide by faith

This, as we have seen, is primary. We 'believed into' Christ, coming to him in faith, and we are to abide in him in exactly the same way. This means keeping fresh our understanding of who he is and what he has done for us. We are to realise what is our present relationship with him and seek to live consistently in light of that. In other words, we are to maintain the posture of faith, reaching towards our Saviour constantly in dependence and trust.

A little child depends on her parents like this. She relies on them for everything—food, clothes, love and protection. Vulnerable as she is, she simply cannot survive in the world without someone stronger and wiser to care for her. We need Christ in the same way. It is only when I can truly say, 'The LORD is my shepherd', that I can be confident that 'I shall not want' (Ps. 23:1).

That Christians are called 'believers' is no accident, for believing is at the heart of our identity. In contrast to the world, we are people who exercise faith in Christ, not just at the beginning of our Christian experience but at every step of the way.

We abide by obedience

This is specifically stated in verse 10: 'If you keep my commandments, you will abide in my love, just as I have kept my Father's commandments and abide in his love.' For Jesus is more than Saviour. He is Lord and God, the one who speaks with supreme authority and whom we are called to obey in all things. To disregard his will is to break fellowship, to separate ourselves from his purposes and blessing. If we are disobeying, we are rejecting and repudiating instead of abiding.

Closeness to Christ comes about in part, therefore, through disciplined, detailed submission to his will. The first psalm begins, 'Blessed is the man', and the Hebrew for 'blessed' is a plural, referring to abounding, multiple blessings—'perfect blessedness', as a metrical version of the psalm has it. But what is this blessedness? Is it an emotional ecstasy or permanent spiritual 'high'? No. Feelings are important, and believers can experience rapturous joy in their relationship with God. But what is described here is something more practical and ethically challenging.

> Blessed is the man who walks not in the counsel of the wicked, nor stands in the way of sinners, nor sits in the seat of scoffers; but his delight is in the law of the LORD, and on his law he meditates day and night.
>
> (Psalm 1:1-2)

Happiness, therefore, can be defined as keeping the commandments. To be obedient to God is not only the path to 'perfect blessedness'; it is blessedness in itself. To obey Christ is to abide in him, to experience his love in its fullness.

But there is more to abiding than faith and obedience. Christ abides in the believer (vv.4,5), and we are told similarly regarding the Father that 'if we love one another, God abides in us' (1 John 4:12). Yet neither Father nor Son obeys or depends on those in whom they abide. There is also a mutual abiding between Father and Son, for, as Christ explains, 'I am in the Father and the Father is in me' (John 14:10). What then is the central element in all these relationships? Something is present which, for us, most certainly includes both trusting and obeying, but which transcends these in bringing us into a deeper experience of abiding.

We abide by communion

To abide in someone is to share with them an inward, enduring personal communion. To converse with them, share ourselves with them and give ourselves to them, to enjoy fellowship on the deepest possible level. This glorious and most satisfying of friendships is both our responsibility and our high privilege.

The Christian practice of daily personal worship is sometimes trivialised into a religious duty, an obligation placed upon us for some reason. We read the Bible and pray regularly because, as young Christians, we were told that this is important. But not everyone grasps what they are really doing and how vital this time is for our Christian living.

It is, in fact, the branch receiving life and strength from the vine, and this life enters our minds and hearts through the Bible. 'If you abide in me,' says Jesus—and he then amplifies and expands on what this involves—'and my words abide in you' (v.7). Each day we are opening ourselves to our Master's words, so that they can fill and mould us. As we read the Scriptures, our Lord is speaking to us with life-changing power. Then, in praise and prayer, we return his words to him—seeking to be brought into line with his will, asking for blessing to flow into us and then out into the world.

Many believers are uncomfortably aware of something lacking in their Christian lives. Perhaps the reason is to be found here. If we are failing to develop our communion with the Lord, how can we expect to enjoy the warmth of his love? How can we be strengthened by a Christ whom we are neglecting? It is not that he has ceased to love us, but that we have ceased to express our love to him. One of the commonest regrets of Christians towards the end of their lives is that they have spent so little time in conscious fellowship with Christ and, if we fail here, we fail everywhere. For J. C. Ryle, this communion lay at the heart of abiding:

> To abide in Christ means to keep up a habit of constant close communion with Him—to be always leaning on Him, resting on Him, pouring out our hearts to Him, and using Him as our Fountain of life and strength, as our chief Companion and best Friend.[32]

We need also, as churches, to focus on communion with the Lord. We must give worship, study and prayer first place in our agenda. Our age is an impatient one, in love with activity, and A. W. Tozer's words are truer now than when he wrote them a generation ago:

> 'The accent in the Church today', says Leonard Ravenhill . . . 'is not on devotion, but on commotion' . . . The adolescent taste which loves the loud horn and thundering exhaust has got into the activities of modern Christians . . . We must begin the needed reform by challenging the spiritual validity of externalism. What a man is must be shown to be more important than what he does . . . We must show a new generation of nervous, almost frantic, Christians that power lies at the center of the life . . . The desire to be dramatically active is proof of our religious infantilism; it is a type of exhibitionism common to the kindergarten.[33]

This is not a plea for quietism, defined in the dictionary as 'a passive attitude towards life, with devotional contemplation and abandonment of the will, as a form of religious mysticism'. It is simply a recognition of the truth of the promise, 'they who wait for the Lord shall renew their strength' (Isa. 40:31). The church which makes a priority of fellowship with Christ will find itself brought by him, as he has promised, to a new level of fruitfulness.

The results which Christ promises

'Whoever abides in me and I in him, he it is that bears much fruit' (v.5). The branch that is securely joined to the vine will bear grapes, for the uninterrupted flow of nourishment from the parent plant inevitably produces fruit. Abiding leads to fruitfulness, as the power of Christ is infused into his people.

What is this fruit? Quite simply, everything that Christ does in us and through us. Christlike character, certainly—'the fruit of the Spirit', described for us in Galatians 5:22-23: 'love, joy, peace, patience, kindness, goodness, faithfulness, gentleness, self-control'. The Lord Jesus changes us into his image, and the fruit we bear is an increasing likeness to him. Such is the wonder of our salvation. God has provided for us that not only are all our sins forgiven, not only are we accepted as righteous in his sight, but we are actually transformed in our very beings, so that more and more we resemble our glorious and beautiful Saviour: 'For those whom he foreknew he also predestined to be conformed to the image of his Son' (Rom. 8:29). Our destiny is to be like the Lord Jesus Christ! What more do we need to fill us with an ecstasy of joy and hope?

Yet the fruit is also effective ministry, reaching out to the world, being used to bring others to Christ, to build them up in their faith, to play a part in extending the kingdom of God. Jesus' original call to his disciples was first of all to union and communion with him, leading inevitably to productive service. '*Follow* me, and *I will make* you become fishers of men', he said (Mark 1:17). Their responsibility was to follow; his was to turn them into fishermen.

We have tended to reverse the responsibilities, giving our attention to how best to fish for the unconverted, what tackle to prepare, what bait to use, what waters to search. But it is Christ's work to 'make' us fishermen, and we should leave it to him. Our task is to devote ourselves to following, remaining close, learning from him and becoming more and more like him. If we concentrate on this, a ministry will come. He will provide us with opportunities for witness, help us to take advantage of them and give the fruit. The same pattern of responsibility, both ours and his, is repeated in Mark 3:14, where we are told of the commissioning of the apostles, 'And he appointed twelve . . . so that *they might be with him and he might send them out.*' First comes our time spent with him, then, as a result, his sending us out.

'Much fruit'—the prospect is thrilling! We are not condemned to second-rate Christian living and service. Christ's will for us is that our lives should be valuable, filled with purpose, that we should make an impact on the world, that our accomplishments on earth should be everlastingly significant. Yet lest, seeing the fruit, we should ever lapse into self-congratulation, this fruit-bearing is linked, as both cause and result, with prayer. 'If you abide in me, and my words abide in you, ask whatever you wish, and it will be done for you' (v.7). Our communion with

73

Christ brings us so into tune with him that in our praying we find ourselves seeking his agenda, not our own, asking in line with his purposes, which have become ours, and thus finding our prayers abundantly answered. Those who do his work in his way discover that, as he builds his church, he is using them in the process.

'Apart from me . . . nothing'

Whether therefore for personal spiritual growth or productive service, abiding is vital. So much so, that the Lord includes a stark warning: 'for apart from me you can do nothing' (v.5). If the link between branch and vine is broken or damaged, so that the branch is 'apart from' the vine, no grapes will appear. It is not simply that we will do no great things, or that we will find it difficult to do something, or achieve it only with enormous pains and effort. 'Nothing' in the original Greek is a double negative, extremely strong—'absolutely nothing of any kind'. Apart from Christ's power working through us, our spiritual achievements will be non-existent.

Is not this a warning which we need to take to heart? How much fruit are we bearing in our personal lives? How much are we accomplishing in our Christian service? Are we really making a significant impact on our world? We must not minimise what God is doing. He is at work—in many places and in wonderful ways. Yet many of the churches, in the Western world at least, are seeing few conversions. Too many of them are dying. Prayer meetings are poorly attended. Evangelistic endeavours produce little apparent fruit. Christ's power is not seen among us in the way that we long for. If we are honest, we must admit this to be the case. And such ineffectiveness is not always attributable to the mysterious, sovereign purposes of God, behind which some half-hearted Christians comfortably shelter. The fault may be ours.

We may be like a vine with many leaves but little fruit. The machinery of the local church hums along as usual. We are busy with various commendable activities and we can delude ourselves into thinking that all is well. But each of us needs to ask, 'What is the Lord Jesus doing in and through me?' Could it be that his verdict on your life or mine, on your church or mine, is 'apart from me . . . nothing'? How terrible to lead a busy yet barren life! To accomplish 'nothing' as Christians would be tragic. Far worse would be to accomplish nothing and not to realise it.

To those who long for greater fruitfulness, the solution is clear. We need to give more attention to cultivating our union with Christ.

> If, then, the will of Christ is not being fulfilled through us, if there is good that it belongs to us to do, but which remains undone, then *the point of juncture with Christ is the point that needs looking to* . . . When we see our leaf fading, when we feel sapless, heartless for Christian duty, reluctant to work for others, to take anything to do in the relief of misery and repression of vice, there is a remedy for this state, and it is to renew our fellowship with Christ.[34]

The encouragement to do this lies in the fact that, if we are Christians, we are not ultimately apart from him, we cannot be. Our 'separation' is due to our failure to experience his grace and enjoy his presence to the degree that we should. The staggering truth is that we are joined for ever to the mighty Lord of glory, the one to whom has been given 'All authority in heaven and on earth' (Matt. 28:18).

'I will build my church', he promised (Matt. 16:18), and he will do it through us to our everlasting gladness, for 'These things I have spoken to you, that my joy may be in you, and that your joy may be full' (v.11).

4
All one in Christ Jesus

So far we have been thinking of life in Christ from the perspective of the individual believer. But it is time, for this chapter at least, to broaden our focus, because this relationship has wider implications.

Coming into Christ brings us at once into the fellowship of a large family— 'the communion of saints', as it is often called. This is classically expressed in a phrase of Paul, where he writes that union with Christ transcends and overcomes all our natural divisions, so that 'There is neither Jew nor Greek, there is neither slave nor free, there is neither male nor female, for you are *all one in Christ Jesus*' (Gal. 3:28).

I was first made aware of this phrase as a boy when I saw it on a banner over a platform in a huge tent on the north coast of Ireland. A Christian conference was taking place, an annual gathering of hundreds of believers from many churches, worshipping together, hearing the Word preached and enjoying fellowship, and this was their motto: 'All one in Christ Jesus'. That week was, and still is, a time of great blessing, and yet the slogan seemed somewhat unreal. For, when the conference had ended, we all went our own way, not to meet again for another year. Christians who might live close together would separate into their own churches, pursue their own activities and have nothing to do with one another until the conference came round again the following summer. 'All one'? It was a beautiful idea; we knew that it was true theoretically, but it seemed irrelevant to daily life. Our 'oneness' had no practical expression. It meant little more than a special annual experience.

As we look at the fragmented state of the wider church, these words can seem even more empty. Christendom is divided into Eastern Orthodoxy, Roman Catholicism and Protestantism. There are sects, cults and 'isms' of every kind. The Protestant churches themselves are split into many denominations, and even these are further sub-divided. How many varieties of Presbyterian or Baptist churches there are! Even within those united by their theology we find various divisions, rivalries and parties. If a person is associated with one particular movement, it is safe to assume that they will have little to do with another grouping which has coalesced elsewhere or is under the influence of a different leader. 'All one'? For our Lord, the unity of the church was to be an essential element in its witness to the world, for he prayed 'that they may all be one . . . so that the world may believe that you have sent me' (John 17:21). Yet his prayer seems further from fulfilment now than when he first offered it.

'But', you may say, 'Paul could write "All one in Christ Jesus" because those were the days of the New Testament church and believers were united then. There were no denominations. Christians were one in a way that is no longer the case and this visible unity made his words appropriate.' Yet was it really like that? Are we sure that the church was seen to be one? Did not Paul write these words to the Corinthians?

I appeal to you, brothers, by the name of our Lord Jesus Christ, that all of you agree and that there be no divisions among you, but that you be united . . . For it

78

has been reported to me . . . that there is quarrelling among you.

(1 Corinthians 1:10,11)

The churches in Galatia and Colossae had been infiltrated by trouble-makers and heretics, and division was the result. The apostle urged the Christians in Rome 'not to quarrel over opinions', not to 'pass judgement on one another any longer' (Rom. 14:1,13). He warned the Ephesian elders that 'after my departure fierce wolves will come in among you, not sparing the flock; and from among your own selves will arise men speaking twisted things, to draw away the disciples after them' (Acts 20:29,30).

While he was thankful for those who preached the gospel in the city of Rome, Paul recognised that some of them were doing so from unworthy motives: 'Some indeed preach Christ from envy and rivalry . . . not sincerely but thinking to afflict me in my imprisonment' (Phil. 1:15,17). At the end of his life of service and sacrifice he was compelled, tragically, to acknowledge that 'all who are in Asia turned away from me' (2 Tim. 1:15). The apostle John, likewise, was aware of schisms in the church, referring to those who 'went out from us, but they were not of us' (1 John 2:19).

We should not look at the New Testament church through rose-coloured spectacles, or imagine that this was a golden period of perfect visible unity. It was not, and the church then was in some respects not so very different from our own. Yet Paul, knowing all this, could write 'you are all one in Christ Jesus'. What does he mean? Is he saying that we will be one some day in heaven? That is certainly true, but it is not what he means here. Is he referring to a unity which is notional only—so idealistic and other-worldly that for all practical purposes we can forget about it? Not at all. The oneness which Paul has in mind is strong, real and substantial.

Louis Berkhof provides a helpful illustration when he writes: 'It [the church] is not a mechanism, in which the parts precede the whole, but an organism, in which the whole is prior to the parts.'[35] That is to say, the church is not a collection of different parts which we have to put together in order to construct a whole. That is what happens with a mechanism. A clockmaker, for example, will gather all the pieces of a clock, painstakingly assemble them and end up with a unity. But the church, says Berkhof, is an organism in which the whole is prior to the parts. A seed is an organism. It will mature and develop, but everything is there in principle from the start. Its growth is merely the outworking of an underlying, pre-existing unity. For the church, that unity is found in union with Christ—we are 'all one in Christ Jesus'.

The dimensions of our oneness in Christ

The unity of Christians is a many-sided reality. There is a paradoxical quality to it, and yet it makes perfect sense. It is complex, yet grounded on a massive simplicity. We will consider seven ways in which the oneness of believers can be seen.

We were all one in Christ before creation

This brings us face to face with the unfathomable mystery of election. In the covenant of redemption, God the Father chose in love a people to be his; God the Son undertook to represent that people in his life and death, and to God the Spirit was allotted the responsibility of creating faith in them so that they might receive the redemption purchased by Christ. God's covenant was instituted before creation, for 'he chose us in him before the foundation of the world' (Eph. 1:4). Jesus refers to this in his 'high-priestly prayer' of John 17, describing his people no fewer than six times as 'those whom you have given me' (John 17:2,6 (twice), 9,12,24). He speaks of them not as a conglomeration of individuals, but as a body, a corporate identity. They are the elect, the chosen, 'those whom you have given me'.

Mystery though it may be, the awesome truth is clear. Our unity is a very ancient thing, older than creation, older than time itself. Before the universe was made, in the counsel of the Triune God, we were all one in Christ Jesus.

We were all one in Christ throughout the Old Testament

As soon as Adam and Eve sinned in Eden, God addressed the devil, prophesying not only judgment but salvation: 'I will put enmity between you and the woman, and between your offspring and her offspring; he shall bruise your head, and you shall bruise his heel' (Gen. 3:15).

God is here creating hostility between two parties—the offsprings of the woman and the serpent, or devil. In the warfare which ensues, the woman's offspring will destroy the offspring of the devil by crushing his head, at the cost of wounding to himself. That offspring, or 'seed' of the woman, is of course the Saviour, but all his people are included in him, and the Old Testament is the story of one people—and how this people is formed, delivered and preserved by God. The membership of the family is to be worldwide, from all the nations, but they look to a common ancestor, to Abraham, to whom God promised that 'in you all the families of the earth shall be blessed' (Gen. 12:3). Paul describes him as 'the father of all who believe . . . the father of us all' (Rom. 4:11,16). One Israel, one chosen people—'all one'.

We were all one in Christ at Calvary

Here is the pivotal event in history, when the Son of God made atonement for sin. But for whom did Christ die? For his people. And how did he regard them? He certainly saw them as individuals. This is a truth precious to every believer, as, with Paul, we look in love and worship to 'the Son of God, who loved me and gave himself for me' (Gal. 2:20). But it is primarily true that Christ saw his people in their totality, as a unity. When Scripture speaks of the objects of his sacrifice, the language is overwhelmingly corporate. 'He will save his people from their sins' (Matt. 1:21). 'I lay down my life for the sheep' (John 10:15). 'Christ loved the church and gave himself up for her' (Eph. 5:25). 'Christ loved *the church*'—the one and only church, universal and united in him.

In his self-offering, Christ held in his mind and affections the whole body of his people throughout history to the end of time. That unity which had been forged in the eternal purpose of God was now sealed by the blood of the Lamb. When we stand at Calvary and look in faith at the Son of God nailed to the wood, we know that we are all one in Christ Jesus.

We are all one in Christ in salvation

There is something inescapably individual about each of our experiences of salvation. My experience is unique. No one has ever been saved or will be saved in exactly the same way as I was, and the same is true for you. One of the joys of eternity may well be listening to the millions of testimonies of God's people as, one after another, they say, 'Come and hear, all you who fear God, and I will tell what he has done for my soul' (Psalm 66:16). What variety there will be! How many accounts of the many-coloured grace of God! For salvation has something uniquely personal about it. Each of us must exercise faith for himself or herself. I must come to Christ as if the only two people in the world were myself and the Saviour. It is an intensely individual transaction.

And we come to faith in so many different ways. Some can never remember a time when they did not love and trust the Lord Jesus. Others come in teenage years or in middle age. Some come easily, some after a prolonged struggle. A few years ago I baptised a man of eighty. He had been as insensible as a stone to spiritual things and we had prayed for years for his salvation. Then, near the end of his life, he was melted, changed by the Spirit of God and through the love, prayers and example of his daughter. For him, all things had become new. What a day that was!

But, however and whenever we come, there is a profound underlying unity. We have all been regenerated, have all repented. We have all trusted in the Saviour and received exactly the same forgiveness. We have all been clothed in the same righteousness and are indwelt by the same Spirit. 'There is one body and one Spirit—just as you were called to the one hope that belongs to your call—one Lord, one faith, one baptism, one God and Father of all, who is over all and through all and in all' (Eph. 4:4-6). In spite of the surface differences, we have all been saved in exactly the same way, all one in Christ Jesus.

We are all one in Christ in our relationship to the Scriptures

The very inspiration and provision of the Bible is a remarkable witness to the unity of believers, for there is one book for all. No matter our nationality, age or temperament, we all read the same Bible. Our circumstances are varied, our needs and our personalities differ, but the same Word is profitable for every Christian who will ever live. Apart from specific commands addressed to particular people—to parents, servants or masters, for example—there is not a syllable of which we can say, 'This applies to others, but not to me.' It applies to us all, no matter when, where or in what situation we may live. There are no exceptions, no special cases, no exclusions. We are all given the same commandments, all blessed with the same promises. We are all one under the authority of the one Book of God.

We are all one in Christ in Christian living

The limitations of the English language obscure the fact that almost all the commands in the New Testament are couched in the second person plural, addressed to a body of people. We have tended to interpret them as being directed solely to the individual believer, but this is a mistake. In normal circumstances, there is no such thing as a solitary Christian, for the Christian life can be lived only in community.

Paul, for example, is constantly speaking of our life together. He is fond of words compounded with 'fellow': 'fellow workers, fellow partners, fellow servants, fellow soldiers, fellow prisoners' (Rom. 16:3; Phil. 1:7; Col. 1:7; Phil. 2:25; Rom. 16:7). Seven of the nine qualities mentioned earlier as characteristic of the fruit of the Spirit (Gal. 5:22,23) require the existence of other believers. We simply cannot practise 'love, patience, kindness, goodness, faithfulness, gentleness, self-control' in solitary splendour. Without other people this fruit of the Spirit cannot develop, so that it is impossible in ordinary circumstances to be a maturing Christian apart from the oneness and interaction of the people of God.

Similarly, how could we obey the frequent New Testament 'one another' commands, such as 'love one another', 'confess your sins to one another' and 'pray for one another' (John 13:34; Jas. 5:16), were there not 'others' around us? The 'one anothers' point to the need for community.

The very duties and assurances of Scripture assume our unity. How often, for example, we hear the various pieces of Christian armour in Ephesians 6 expounded in individualistic terms! The picture implied is of a single soldier, marching out alone against the enemy. But what general would fight a war in this way, and what success could he expect? How much more sense the passage makes when we realise that, although there is an application to the individual fighter, the general picture is that of Christ's army going to war together! The verbs are plural. It is as a body, a people, that we are to 'fasten on the belt of truth . . . put on the breastplate of righteousness . . . and take the helmet of salvation, and the sword of the Spirit' (Eph. 6:14ff).

The fabric of church life itself—worship, prayer, evangelism—is set in a corporate context. So much emphasis has been given to our private devotions that it comes as a surprise to contemporary Christians to hear that previous generations considered public worship a greater means of blessing than private.[36] There is a togetherness about the New Testament church which we are losing in our impersonal, atomistic world. Christian living, biblically understood, is predicated on the existence of the people of God.

We are all one in Christ in glory

Now we have come full circle, for we began in eternity and that is where we end. We were all one in Christ before the world was, and we will still be all one in Christ when this earth has passed away. God chose us in love before creation, and he will gather us together in love at the consummation. As the Lord Jesus put it, 'This is the will of him who sent me, that I should lose nothing of all that he has given me, but raise it up on the last day' (John 6:39). John's vision in Revelation is a glorious one:

> After this I looked, and behold, a great multitude that no one could number, from every nation, from all tribes and peoples and languages, standing before the throne and before the Lamb, clothed in white robes, with palm branches in their hands, and crying out with a loud voice, 'Salvation belongs to our God who sits on the throne, and to the Lamb!'
>
> (Revelation 7:9,10)

This is not idealistic dreaming, but a monumental, rock-like reality. Our oneness in Christ is a fact, demonstrated in a multitude of ways. Christian unity is massive in its dimensions. Our identity is the same. Our experience is the same. Our destiny is the same. We are all one in Christ Jesus. But what does this mean for us in practice?

The implications of our oneness in Christ

The fact that we are one in Christ has a number of practical implications. We will consider six of these.

The limitation

This unity has boundaries, a dividing-line, a condition which must be met if the unity is to be experienced. 'All one *in Christ Jesus*.' For we are all one, but in Christ and only in him. There is no unity outside the Lord Jesus. He is the great reality upon which our oneness is based, the basis of our unity. We are united only with those who, like us, are hooked to his belt. He is the vine and we are the branches. He is the head of the body and we are the members. His life runs in our veins. His will directs us. This is the limitation—'in Christ Jesus'.

Those, therefore, who are not in Christ are not one with us. They are still in Adam, and between us and them is a vast gulf. They may claim to be one with us, may profess to be part of the Church—and be recognised as such by others. But they do not meet the basic requirement, for it is impossible for someone not joined to the head to be part of the body.

This obvious truth destroys at one stroke much of the twentieth-century ecumenical movement. For the fatal weakness of that drive for church unity was that its advocates fudged the main issue. They never faced up to basic questions such as, 'Who or what is a Christian? How can we distinguish between a true and a false Christian?' Instead, they took such matters for granted. They never asked, 'What is the mark of being in Christ?', but assumed that all who profess to be in Christ are in Christ, and that the unity of all who claim to be Christians is that unity for which the Lord prayed.

This confusion led Professor John Murray to describe the modern movement for church unity as 'a monstrous travesty'[37] of what Christ was praying for, and it lies at the root of its almost total failure. For it has failed—publicly and embarrassingly. In the 1960s the Christian world was dominated by the activities and aims of the World Council of Churches. Enormous publicity was given to its efforts to build one world church. What has happened to it now? It has dwindled into insignificance. Of course! It was never more than an ecclesiastical tower of Babel, a man-made striving after unity which had no foundation in God's truth.

This limitation to those truly 'in Christ Jesus' means that, at times, we have to make hard choices. At a local level, the faithful minister will have to distance himself and his people from some inter-church gatherings and ecumenical get-togethers. He may well be branded a bigot, a prejudiced Pharisee. 'What is wrong with you?', people will say. 'All the Christians in the town are meeting together and you think you are too good to meet with the rest of us!'

But that is not the case at all. If only it were the case that all the Christians in the town were getting together! The problem is that they are not all Christians, and it would be a betrayal of our Lord and of his Word to sit on a platform with someone who denies the gospel and call him a brother. On some moral and civic issues, we may be able to co-operate with people of any faith and none, but if it ever means accepting someone as a Christian who does not profess the true faith, we cannot do it. We separate ourselves, not because we are uninterested in Christian unity, but for precisely the opposite reason. We take with the utmost seriousness what Christian unity really is.

There is a searching question here for believers who remain in denominations where unbelief is propagated and defended, where some ministers are known as 'liberals' and some congregations as 'non-evangelical', where biblical church discipline is almost non-existent. Can God's people who remain in such bodies say with a good conscience that they are living out true Christian unity? Paul's instruction to young Christians was categorical: 'As we have said before, so now I say again: If anyone is preaching to you a gospel contrary to the one you received, let him be accursed' (Gal. 1:9). Are you really treating false teachers as 'accursed' if they are recognised as ministers in good standing in the church to which you belong? Is your association with them not a betrayal of the crucial limitation?

The challenge comes also to each of us as individuals. Am I truly in Christ? Or am I still in a different category, still outside him, still not trusting? Do you belong? Are you 'in Christ Jesus', so that you are part of the 'all one'?

The comprehensiveness

But note here the beautiful balance of the teaching of Scripture. There is unity only in Christ. Yet it is equally true that there is unity always in Christ. This is why Paul, writing to the Corinthians, could write at the same time to 'all those who in every place call upon the name of our Lord Jesus Christ, both their Lord and ours' (1 Cor. 1:2). The very faithfulness to Christ which prevents us from uniting with those who do not belong to him requires us to recognise as brothers and sisters all those who are his.

Here is the breadth, the generosity of Christian unity. It transcends all man-made boundaries of race, class, culture and nationality. It overleaps all human divisions, sometimes very painful ones. Simon the Zealot and Matthew the tax-collector, at opposite poles of the political spectrum, were brothers in Christ. Before they met Jesus, Simon might have wanted to cut Matthew's throat, but when the Master called them to himself, they served him together. Similarly, Paul could explain to young Christians that in Christ 'there is not Greek and Jew, circumcised and uncircumcised, barbarian, Scythian, slave, free; but Christ is all, and in all' (Col. 3:11).

Our unity in Christ cannot be contained within denominational boundaries. We have, of course, disagreements with fellow Christians, some of them serious ones. If they and we are in Christ, however, we are brothers and sisters, no matter how significant the issues that divide us. We must do our best not to be defensive, timid or narrow. We must not stay aloof from fellow believers as if they might contaminate us in some awful way. We are to see Christ's church as Christ himself sees it. As he said to Peter when the apostle was questioning the wideness of God's mercy, 'What God has made clean, do not call common' (Acts 10:15).

Some Christians are hard for us to relate to. We may find their ways of worship alien and their lifestyle disturbing; we may consider some of their doctrines misguided. We may be right! But, if they are true Christians, our Lord loved and loves them. For them he was willing to die on the cross and they will be with us for ever in heaven. It is perilously easy to develop, and even take pride in, an 'Elijah complex'. You remember how the great prophet, in a mood of discouragement, cried out, 'I, even I only, am left' (1 Kings 19:10). We too, either from arrogance or disappointment, can tend to think that of ourselves. But God assured his servant that there were in Israel thousands of faithful believers of whose existence he had been quite unaware. So it is with us. In your locality and mine are many who love the Lord Jesus as we do. When we think of the breadth and extent of the church we should thank God and take courage.

We need also to remember that each of us has a temperamental imbalance towards one extreme or another, overstressing either the limitation or the comprehensiveness. Some of us may be too narrow in our sympathies, too ready to exclude others from our fellowship. Others of us may be a little too warm-hearted, even woolly-minded perhaps, and ready to accept everyone who makes a profession. We need to recognise our particular area of weakness, to realise the particular extreme towards which we tend, and seek to correct it.

The diversity

Although there is unity in Christ, this is not uniformity, not dreary sameness. Just as, when God created the world, he adorned it with an endless variety of plants and animals, so is there astonishing variety in the body of Christ, since, as the Church Fathers said, 'grace follows nature'. The body of Christ is not monochrome, it is not—fashionable but horrible word!—'homogeneous'. Who in their right mind would want to be part of a homogeneous church? Part of the beauty of God's grace is the variety of its working— different types of people, different temperaments, different gifts, different experiences.

This is one of the distinctions between a church and a cult. In a cult, the members seem programmed, robotic. They quote the same Scriptures, respond in the same way, follow exactly the same path. Even in some churches with an over-dominant leader we see this phenomenon, as everyone tries to imitate the pastor. But the church is meant to be diverse. This is part of its witness, for it is saying to the world, 'Here is a group of people so varied and so different from each other that the only explanation for them staying together is the grace and power of God.'

The glory of this diversity is that, far from being divisive, it enhances our unity. This is Paul's argument in his teaching on the church as the body of Christ: 'For the body does not consist of one member but of many . . . If all were a single member, where would the body be? As it is, there are many parts, yet one body' (1 Cor. 12:14,19-20). We need the foot, the hand, the ear and the eye. They are all different, but that is precisely the point. We need each other, not in spite of our differences but because of them. This unity in diversity enables us both to appreciate our fellow believers and to properly value ourselves. The doctrine of the body means that we can never say to another Christian, 'You are no good. I do not need you.' Nor can we say of ourselves, 'I am no good. They don't need me.'

Can we go further and say that, in the providence of God, the existence of separate denominations may not be an entirely bad thing? Is it possible that God has used them at different times in history to maintain certain truths, keep certain emphases alive, specialise in doctrines which the rest of the church was neglecting? Whether or not that is the case, we should give thanks for the diversity of the body of Christ. As a minister I may, at times, feel that some of our members are rather more diverse than is comfortable and wish for a little more uniformity! But I know in my heart that it is in our differences that our strength lies. The dazzling diversity will not end with this life but will continue in heaven, in the 'great multitude . . . from every nation, from all tribes and peoples and languages' (Rev. 7:9). We will not be absorbed in some bland common denominator, but will bring our grace-enhanced uniqueness, our personalities, perhaps even our national characteristics, before the throne of God.

The God-centredness

It may be weakness on my part, but I simply cannot get excited about certain forms of ecclesiastical diplomacy. In the course of my ministry I have seen various schemes put forward for union between true Christians. Alliances have been formed, federations planned, councils set up. Their proponents have been enthusiastic, well-meaning, filled with glowing hope. 'This will be the end', they say,

'of divisions. This will make us all one in Christ Jesus.'
All has come to nothing, and largely, I believe, because
of its flawed perspective and disproportionate self-
importance.

For the thinking behind such attempts seems to be that
the church of Christ is fragmented and broken, and it is up
to us to put it together again. But, as we have seen, that is
simply not true. We have noted what God has done, we
have marvelled at the depth and permanence of the unity
he has created. We were one before creation, were one at
Calvary, will still be one in glory. He has taken us out of
Adam and brought us into Christ. He will do it!

This is not to say that we should decry efforts at building visible unity, and we will come to that in a moment.
But we should never take ourselves and our little efforts
too seriously. God has a mighty unifying purpose for the
world, 'to unite all things in him [Christ], things in
heaven and things on earth' (Eph. 1:10), and this purpose
is being carried out and will be brought to complete fulfilment. We need to relax, knowing that Christ is building
his church into a unity which is, and will be seen to be,
all his doing.

The challenge
But, and here again is the balance of Scripture which
almost at times seems to lead us to contradict ourselves, we
do need to realise that we also have a duty to make our
oneness in Christ more visible. John Murray has strong
words to say about failure to pursue this goal:

> While spurious unity is to be condemned, the lack of
> unity among churches of Christ which profess the faith
> in its purity is a patent violation of the unity of the body
> of Christ, and of that unity which the prayer of our Lord

requires us to promote. We cannot escape from the implications for us by resorting to the notion of the invisible church. The body of Christ is not an invisible entity, and the prayer of Jesus was directed to the end that the world might believe . . . What needs to be indicted . . . with vehemence is the complacency so widespread, and the failure to be aware that this is an evil, dishonouring to Christ . . . and prejudicial to the evangelistic outreach to the world.[38]

We need to grieve over the divisions of the church and seek to heal them wherever possible. And what about those wretched splits! Congregations fighting and dividing! Denominations arguing and dividing! The world laughs and the demons cheer. Almost invariably, those involved insist that the division is over a matter of principle. But that is very rarely the case. It is usually a matter of sin, of self-centredness and pride. Any good resulting from the division is outweighed by the damage it inflicts upon the cause of Christ.

We should have the ambition of being peacemakers in the church. We should be willing to submerge our prejudices, allow ourselves to be overruled, take a back seat, forgive, forgive and forgive again. We need to pray for long-suffering and patience, to resolve that we will do nothing to disturb the unity of the people of God. Where division exists, J. C. Ryle's recipe for good relations still applies: 'Keep the walls of separation as low as possible, and shake hands over them as often as you can.'[39]

The means
How do we reach this fuller unity? How do we develop and maintain it? The answer is simple, though not easy. Who

made us one? Christ. How then can we come closer together? By coming closer to Christ. The classic illustration is the cartwheel. We are the spokes in the wheel and Christ is the hub. As each spoke gets nearer to the hub, so it becomes closer to all the others. So the nearer we grow to Christ, the closer we will become to our brothers and sisters.

Unity, in other words, should never be sought as our prime goal. C. S. Lewis called his spiritual autobiography *Surprised by Joy*, because he discovered that, to find joy, you have to forget about it and let it take you by surprise as you seek God. So it is with Christian unity. It takes us by surprise as we seek Christ the centre, as we seek an ever greater measure of his Spirit. This is not escapism or an excuse for doing nothing. It is the simple truth. It is Christ who unites us, and the deeper our love for him, the deeper our love for one another.

'All one in Christ Jesus.' It speaks to a deep longing in the human heart, for God himself said of the crown of his creation, 'It is not good that the man should be alone' (Gen. 2:18). May Christ teach us to love one another, and may that love be experienced more and more among us. 'Behold, how good and pleasant it is when brothers dwell in unity! . . . For there the Lord has commanded the blessing, life for evermore' (Ps. 133:1,3).

5
The fellowship of
his sufferings

We are born to suffer. It is a given in human existence, and the fact that we may be Christians provides us with no immunity from pain, for Paul reminds us that 'through many tribulations we must enter the kingdom of God' (Acts 14:22). We suffer physically, from various bodily aches and ailments. We suffer mentally, from anxiety, frustration or depression. We suffer from life's disappointments and injustices. We suffer from those who do not wish us well and, sometimes, from our friends. No one is exempt from suffering. It is a characteristic feature of life in this world.

How do we react to our suffering? Do we become bitter and cynical? Do we grow disappointed with God, thinking that he has been unfair to us, that he has let us down in some way? Are we angry with him because of the hurts he has allowed us to experience? Do we ever wonder if our problem is that we are not claiming the 'abundant life' which, we are assured by its proponents, should be ours in Christ? Have we been influenced by the claims of the so-called 'health and wealth gospel', which tells us that, if we have enough faith, we can be set free from suffering of every kind? Such nonsense is doubly cruel, because it leaves those who believe it not only disillusioned when illness does not disappear, but guilty as well, because they are held to be to blame for the absence of healing. I can still remember my rage when a Christian woman came to me in tears. Her daughter was seriously disabled and another believer had in effect said to her, 'It is your fault that your daughter is as she is, your lack of faith which is keeping her in this condition.'

Or, as is, I suppose, the case with most of us, do we put up with our suffering as best we can, realising that it is part of the 'not yet' of living in a fallen world, and that we are experiencing 'the sufferings of this present time' which 'are not worth comparing with the glory that is to be revealed to us' (Rom. 8:18)? This is a sane, biblical way to regard our sufferings, and yet in itself it is incomplete. For we need to go deeper, and one of the best ways of doing this is to see our sufferings through the lens of union with Christ.

But what relevance can this have to our troubles? At first sight, it might seem to contradict them, to make the problem of suffering even more perplexing. Since it is true that we have been brought into the closest connection with the reigning, triumphant Lord, should we then be weak and in pain? Yet that apparently is the case, for Scripture in several places explicitly links our sufferings with our union with Christ. Peter urges us to 'rejoice insofar as you share Christ's sufferings' (1 Pet. 4:13). Paul writes that we are 'fellow heirs with Christ, provided we suffer with him' (Rom. 8:17), and again that 'we share abundantly in Christ's sufferings' (2 Cor. 1:5). In fact, he goes further and tells us that it is his ambition to share these sufferings: 'that I may know him and the power of his resurrection, and may share his sufferings, becoming like him in his death' (Phil. 3:10). Far from contradicting each other, the two realities seem to belong together.

How can this be? In what sense does union with Christ help us to see our sufferings in a new light? There are four ways in which it is relevant.

Evidence of our identity in Christ

Many people admire Jesus Christ in a vague, general way. They regard him as a good man, a superb teacher, an inspiring example. But when he was on earth he was not widely admired. Instead, he was hated and murdered. If he were to return to this world in the same way as he once came, he would be hated and murdered again.

For God said that he would put enmity not only between Christ and the devil but between their two offsprings (Gen. 3:15), and this enmity has existed ever since. Satan hates Christ and therefore hates those who are in Christ. Our Lord warned his followers of this:

> If the world hates you, know that it has hated me before it hated you . . . Remember the word that I said to you: 'A servant is not greater than his master. If they perse-cuted me, they will also persecute you.'
>
> (John 15:18,20)

Paul quoted the psalmist's plaintive cry to God, 'For your sake we are being killed all the day long' (Rom. 8:36).

As Christians, then, we need not expect to be popular. We should not be obnoxious or offensive of course, as, regrettably, some Christians can be. But we need to be realistic. The world is not waiting to welcome us with open arms. There is no widespread hunger for the gospel. We are told that this is a tolerant age, but the one thing the world will not tolerate is the dogmatism of God's Word. Our culture proclaims its desire to be sensitive towards minorities and to do everything possible to avoid offend-ing their susceptibilities. No one in the media would dare to make fun of Allah, the god of Islam. Advocates of weird or perverted ideas are listened to with unwarranted respect. Yet the name of our blessed Saviour is constantly blasphemed, and evangelical believers in particular are considered fair game for misrepresentation and scorn. There is a venomous hatred of Christianity bubbling beneath the surface of our society, and this satanically inspired enmity is showing signs of erupting ever more aggressively.

In 1 Corinthians, Paul, speaking primarily of the apostles but including by implication all Christians, makes a grim but all too accurate assessment: 'We have become, and are still, like the scum of the world, the refuse of all things' (1 Cor. 4:13). That word 'refuse' referred in ordinary speech to the grease and grime which was scraped from the body in the bath. What a description of how the world regards us! We must expect opposition, hatred, suffering—even persecution. We should not be taken aback by these things. They are evidence of our identity in Christ, proof that we are truly 'in him'.

We should, in fact, be worried if we find ourselves too popular in the world. 'Woe to you,' said Christ, 'when all people speak well of you' (Luke 6:26), for such popularity is a sign that we are not clearly seen to be Christlike. To the believer, the applause of the world is a shameful and humiliating thing. This is why we can rejoice in suffering, for it assures us that we belong to Christ, that we stand with him outside the camp (Heb. 13:13).

Suffering for our Lord's sake means that we are part of a noble company, for he encouraged his disciples to 'Rejoice and be glad . . . for so they persecuted the prophets who were before you' (Matt. 5:12). It is evidence that we have been taken out of Adam. 'If you were of the world,' the Lord said, 'the world would love you as its own; but because you are not of the world, but I chose you out of the world, therefore the world hates you' (John 15:19). Persecution is the devil's compliment, proof that he takes us seriously.

To suffer in this way, furthermore, is a privilege, a sign of future glory, as Peter reminded his apprehensive readers: 'Rejoice insofar as you share Christ's sufferings, that you may also rejoice and be glad when his glory is revealed' (1 Pet. 4:13). Or, in Paul's words, 'We are . . . heirs of God and fellow heirs with Christ, provided we suffer with him in order that we may also be glorified with him' (Rom. 8:17).

When Paul speaks of suffering, he knows what he is talking about. For this is no mere theoretician writing from the comfort of a study. He knew what it was to be stripped to the waist and have his back torn open with the dreaded thirty-nine lashes. One whipping could kill a man, and Paul experienced it five times! On three other occasions he was beaten with Roman rods and was stoned at least once (2 Cor. 11:24,25).

Towards the end of his letter to the Galatians he makes a fascinating comment: 'From now on let no one cause me trouble, for I bear on my body the marks of Jesus' (Gal. 6:17). There was a controversy in those churches about circumcision, a mark on the body. False teachers had come in and, because Paul did not insist on circumcision for all believers, they accused him of not caring about the vital mark on the body. So it seems as if he is saying here, 'You Judaizers make a great fuss about a mark on the body. Let me show you my scarred, ruined back. These are the marks on the body which count—marks of faithfulness to my Lord.'

The wounds and scars we receive in the service of our Master are medals of honour, evidence of our union with the One who was despised and rejected by men. They are proof of our identity in Christ.

Pattern of our conformity to Christ

Jesus Christ is not only our Saviour. He is also, in a profound, structural sense, our pattern. For his life and death not only achieve our salvation but provide its shape, which is that of a parabola. He came down to earth, died and was buried, rose again and ascended into glory, and this is the model for our experience of salvation. Hooked to his belt, we go down with him, only to rise again. In order to be saved, we have to be convicted and broken. We are brought down deep, humbled, filled with repentance for our sin. Then, and only then, we are lifted up in the power of his resurrection to the joy of everlasting glory.

Our sanctification also begins with a negative element, a downward movement: 'Consider yourselves dead to sin.' It then moves on to the positive, the upward: 'and alive to God in Christ Jesus' (Rom. 6:11). We implement this realisation by the daily practice of dying to sin and living to righteousness, and the initial experience is always painful.

God makes us holy by means of suffering. Our Lord was perfectly holy, and yet we are told that 'Although he was a son, he learned obedience through what he suffered' (Heb. 5:8). The meaning is not that he had to learn to be obedient, for he had never been anything else. It is rather that Christ, through what he suffered during his earthly life, experienced the taste and feel, as it were, of what obeying God involves. So do we. Obedience is not something which can be learned in theory. It has to be lived.

When, in other words, we ask God to make us more Christlike, we should tremble as we make that request. 'Lord,' we pray, 'I have an unforgiving spirit. Please make me a more forgiving person.' How will God answer that prayer? By surrounding us with wonderfully kind people who do us nothing but good? No, we become forgiving people by practising forgiveness. So God will allow us to be hurt, criticised and wronged by others, and it is in the pain of working through this and learning to forgive them freely from the heart that we are changed and our prayer is answered.

We become meek as others metaphorically slap us across the face and elbow us out of the way. We learn patience by having to wait, wearily and long. God makes us more loving by bringing into our lives individuals who are unpleasant and difficult to love. Our faith is strengthened during those times when the Lord takes away the props we have been leaning on and brings us into places of darkness and fear. In the words of John Calvin,

> For whomever the Lord has adopted . . . ought to prepare themselves for a hard, toilsome, and unquiet life, crammed with very many and various kinds of evil . . . Beginning with Christ, his first-born, he follows this plan with all his children.[40]

This is the pattern of our conformity to Christ, this is how he blesses us by answering our prayers. It is how he makes us more like his Son. As Sinclair Ferguson has put it, 'Conformity to the risen Christ is possible only when conformity to the crucified Christ is present.'[41] And it is this which explains the strange order of Paul's longing in Philippians 3:10: 'that I may know him and the power of his resurrection, and may share his sufferings, becoming like him in his death'. Resurrection—then suffering? Surely it should be the other way round? But Paul is telling us that, as we live a new life in the risen Christ, he leads us to 'share his sufferings' so that we may at the end 'attain the resurrection from the dead' (Phil. 3:11). It is the parabola again. We go down so that we may rise. The triumphalist model of the Christian life, so popular in many places today, is false, for it is by suffering that we are made more like our Saviour.

The same process is being worked out in our physical bodies. We are weak, ageing and dying, not in spite of being joined to Christ but because of our union with him. The 'super-spiritual' in Corinth despised Paul because of his unimpressive physical appearance. 'His bodily presence is weak', they said (2 Cor. 10:10). Paul could have answered by pointing to the glory that was to come, but he understands instead that his frailty is not a contradiction but a proof of his being in Christ: 'For we also are weak *in him*' (2 Cor. 13:4)—'always carrying in the body the death of Jesus' (2 Cor. 4:10).

What a refreshing way to look at our grey hairs and walking sticks, our aching joints and contact lenses! For even the youngest of us will come to this eventually. In one sense, of course, they are the result of sin's entry into the world, but in another they are part of the pattern of our likeness to Christ. We are joined to the One who died in weakness and was raised in power. His body suffered and so do ours. His body died, so will ours. Our physical weakness is an outward reflection of the parabola of grace in the soul. Down we go, up we will rise. 'He who raised the Lord Jesus will raise us also with Jesus' (2 Cor. 4:14). Here is the pattern of our conformity to Christ.

Necessity in our service of Christ

Christ's suffering was not just an inevitable by-product of his coming to earth. It is not the case that he had a great work to accomplish, but that this coincidentally involved collateral suffering. No, suffering was his task, the reason for his incarnation. It was at the heart of his mission, as 'he humbled himself by becoming obedient to the point of death, even death on a cross' (Phil. 2:8).

It was through suffering that he obtained forgiveness for our sins and brought us eternal life. As the offspring of the woman, he was destined to overcome the devil, but he achieved this by crushing his enemy's head with his heel, which had to be bruised in the process (Gen. 3:15). At Calvary he triumphed, finishing the work which the Father had given him to do. But the cross was for him the place of utmost and unparalleled agony. He had to seem to be defeated in order to triumph. His suffering was not an accompaniment to his ministry, but the essence of his work and at the heart of his victory.

As the body of Christ, we are to continue his work in the world, and we do it as he did—by suffering. This pain begins in our own hearts as, by the Spirit's enabling, we put to death our besetting sins, say no to temptation, deny ourselves daily. It hurts! How much easier it would be to compromise and yield to the devil's temptings. But, what-ever the cost, we are to fight the bloody, lifelong battle against indwelling sin. Such inward suffering is at the heart of our commitment to Christ.

Similarly, we cannot serve him faithfully without suf-fering. The work of the church is often demanding and dif-ficult. We can give ourselves wholeheartedly to some piece of Christian service, yet see no apparent fruit, even after many years. We grow tired, become discouraged occasion-ally, sometimes feel like giving up. But disciples do not give up. It is not an option for us. To take the gospel to the lost can be frustrating, even terrifying at times. Caring for people, making ourselves available for them, will drain us, exhaust us, break our hearts. Desperate moments will come when we say, 'I simply can't go on.' But we do go on. Taking a public stand for the Lord Jesus will bring down on our heads the antagonism of a God-rejecting world. But these things must be faced if we are to be loyal to our Master.

There is no cost-free, comfortable way to serve Christ. The way of discipleship is the way of the cross, and this is a note which, in our day, is not being sounded clearly enough. Too many professing believers are self-indulgent, cowardly, reluctant to put themselves on the line for the Lord. They seem to be 'lovers of pleasure rather than lovers of God, having the appearance of godliness, but denying its power' (2 Tim. 3:4,5).

But when Christ calls a man to follow him, he calls him to come and die, for 'whoever does not take his cross and follow me is not worthy of me' (Matt. 10:38). Paul understood this when he linked his sufferings and his service, describing the pastorate as 'in my flesh . . . filling up what is lacking in Christ's afflictions for the sake of his body, that is, the church' (Col. 1:24). For us, too, to minister is to suffer—a necessity in our Christian service.

Channel for our communion with Christ

Union with Christ is not just a legal arrangement, an abstract theory. As we have seen in the imagery of the vine and the branches, it is something to be known, nurtured and developed. This happens through worship, through obedience, through conscious communion—but also through a shared experience of suffering. Paul has this in mind when he speaks of his longing to 'share his sufferings' (Phil. 3:10)—or, more literally, 'to know the fellowship of his sufferings'.

For there is a fellowship in suffering. Those who have passed through the same painful experience have something in common. Listen to people who find that they have gone through war together or suffered from an identical illness or had the same operation. They may just have met for the first time, but in a few moments they are talking like old friends. Their suffering brings them closer to each other. An instinctive bond unites them.

In exactly the same way our sufferings can bring us closer to Christ and help us to know him better. They open a window into his earthly life and enable us to enter into his experience. He speaks in the Psalms, for example, of 'those who hate me without cause'. 'I have become a stranger to my brothers', he says. 'I looked . . . for comforters, but I found none' (Ps. 69:4,8,20). You may be able to identify with that. Perhaps you are the only Christian in your family, and in your own home you are misunderstood and there is a distance there, an aching loneliness.

Or think of the dark and terrifying hour when Jesus prayed, 'My Father, if it be possible, let this cup pass from me' (Matt. 26:39). Faced with some dreadful cup, you too may have prayed that prayer with all your heart and soul. When you read that 'In the days of his flesh, Jesus offered up prayers and supplications, with loud cries and tears, to him who was able to save him from death' (Heb. 5:7), you can remember times when you too have wept, and so you realise that you know him better than before.

These shared experiences furnish us with a deeper insight into the heart and mind of our Lord. They give us a 'fellow feeling'. Somehow, he becomes more close, more real to us. We understand what Paul meant when he said, 'that I may know him . . . and may share his sufferings' (Phil. 3:10).

But what is even more wonderful—because communion is never a one-way thing—is that not only do our sufferings give us a better understanding of our Saviour's experience, but they also evoke in a very special way his tender care for us. For Christ is in no way uninvolved or remote from us. His sympathy reaches down to his suffering people. Paul learned this on the road to Damascus, when the risen Lord asked, 'Saul, Saul, why are you persecuting *me*?' (Acts 9:4). Had Saul been persecuting Jesus? Surely it had been men and women in Jerusalem and other places—ordinary little people, but not Jesus of Nazareth. 'No', said the Saviour. 'They are part of me. When you touch them, you touch me. When you persecute them, you persecute me. Their sufferings become mine.' 'I am Jesus whom you are persecuting' (Acts 26:15).

This identification had been prophesied centuries before, when Isaiah had written of the Lord, 'In all their affliction he was afflicted' (Isa. 63:9). It lies behind Jesus' teaching on the final judgement, when he will say to those who cared for hungry, thirsty, sick and imprisoned believers, 'as you did it to one of the least of these my brothers, you did it to me' (Matt. 25:40). This is the union between Christ and his people.

And we need to grasp it. 'Does Christ love all his people equally?' we sometimes ask. Well, in a sense of course he does, for he has no favourites in his family. He loves us all, perfectly, infinitely and intensely. But there is another sense in which his love is not always manifested equally to all his children.

Think of a human family with, let us say, four children. The parents love all their children equally—they make no

difference between them, nor should they. But on a particular occasion one of the children is ill—crying, fretful and
distressed. Is it not the case that, although father and
mother love all in exactly the same way, in this crisis there
is one child who is the special focus of their most tender
care and attention? They devote themselves especially to
this little one and make allowances and provide extra
treats. And the other children do not take it badly, for they
understand that their brother or sister is not well, and
mummy and daddy need to look after them.

That is how we should think of the Lord Jesus Christ.
The writer of the letter to the Hebrews, for example,
assures us repeatedly of his special love and help for those
who are in need.

> For we do not have a high priest who is unable to sym-
> pathize with our weaknesses . . . For because he himself
> has suffered when tempted, he is able to help those who
> are being tempted.
>
> (Hebrews 4:15; 2:18)

All over the world are hurting Christians—lonely, broken-
hearted, in pain, persecuted, imprisoned—and the Lord's
great heart is moved with pity towards them, so that there
is from him to them a peculiar outpouring of his affection
and grace.

If you are a believer in need, be sure of your Saviour's
love—hold on to the truth that he knows your pain and is
reaching out to you now in compassion and mercy. All
that suffering can do, if you respond to it in faith, is drive
you closer to Jesus, make you even more dear to him,
lead him to uphold you in passionate affection. 'Let us
then with confidence draw near to the throne of grace,

that we may receive mercy and find grace to help in time of need' (Heb. 4:16).

Our communion with Christ is so intimate and all-embracing that he loves even the dust into which our bodies dissolve. After life on earth has ended, we are 'the dead in Christ' (1 Thess. 4:16). We die 'to the Lord' (Rom. 14:8) and 'in the Lord' (Rev. 14:13). The Shorter Catechism puts it beautifully when it tells us of believers, whose souls at death have been made perfect in holiness, that *'their bodies, being still united to Christ*, do rest in their graves, till the resurrection'.[42] The Heidelberg Catechism sets forth this truth in the answer to its very first question, 'What is thy only comfort in life and death? That I *with body and soul*, both in life and death, am not my own, but belong unto my faithful Saviour Jesus Christ.'[43]

'Union' is an abstract noun and 'union with Christ' is a theologians' term. It can appear impersonal and academic, but there is nothing cold about our union with Christ. It is the language of love, of intimacy. It speaks to us of safety, security and overwhelming joy. We are in Christ and he is in us.

What awaits us in the future? In the long term, heaven. In the short term, who of us can tell? But of one thing we can be sure: the Lord Jesus will never leave those who are united to him.

> For I am sure that neither death nor life, nor angels nor rulers, nor things present nor things to come, nor powers, nor height nor depth, nor anything else in all creation, will be able to separate us from the love of God in Christ Jesus our Lord.
>
> (Romans 8:38-39)

Notes

1. John Murray, *Redemption Accomplished and Applied* (Grand Rapids, Eerdmans, 1955), p. 161.
2. Sinclair B. Ferguson, *The Holy Spirit* (Leicester, Inter-Varsity Press, 1996), p. 100.
3. Thomas Goodwin, 'Christ Set Forth', *Works*, vol. iv (Edinburgh, The Banner of Truth Trust, 1979 edition), p. 31.
4. Westminster Shorter Catechism, 16.
5. George Smeaton, *Christ's Doctrine of the Atonement* (Edinburgh, The Banner of Truth Trust, 1991 edition), p. 65.
6. From 'Praise to the Holiest in the Height', by John Henry Newman.
7. Westminster Shorter Catechism, 30.
8. Robert L. Dabney, *Systematic Theology* (Edinburgh, The Banner of Truth Trust, 1985), p. 615.
9. Ferguson, *The Holy Spirit*, pp. 101,102.
10. John Calvin, *Commentary on 1 Corinthians*, on 1:5, quoted in Ferguson, p. 101.
11. John Owen, 'On Communion with God', *Works*, vol. 2 (London, The Banner of Truth Trust, 1965), p. 32.
12. Westminster Shorter Catechism, 35.
13. John Murray, *The Epistle to the Romans*, vol. 1 (London, Marshall, Morgan & Scott, 1960), p. 225.
14. Leon Morris, *The Epistle to the Romans* (Leicester, Inter-Varsity Press, 1988), p. 255.
15. John R. W. Stott, *The Message of Romans* (Leicester, Inter-Varsity Press, 1994), p. 180.
16. James Philip, *The Power of God* (Edinburgh, Didasko, 1987), p. 97.
17. John Owen, *Works*, vol. 6, p. 9.
18. Walter Marshall, *The Gospel Mystery of Sanctification* (London, James Duncan, 1836), Direction IX, p. 124.
19. James S. Stewart, *A Man in Christ* (London, Hodder & Stoughton, 1935), pp. 168,169.
20. John Murray, *The Epistle to the Romans*, vol. 1, p. 227.

21. Stewart, *A Man in Christ*, p. 199.
22. John Owen, 'Of the Dominion of Sin and Grace', *Works*, vol. 7, p. 560.
23. James Fraser, *A Treatise on Sanctification* (Old Paths Publications, 1992), p. 78.
24. D. Martyn Lloyd-Jones, *Romans: The New Man* (London, The Banner of Truth Trust, 1972), p. 174.
25. J. I. Packer, *Keep in Step With the Spirit* (Leicester, Inter-Varsity Press, 1984), p. 157.
26. Lloyd-Jones, *Romans: The New Man*, p. xii.
27. Stewart, *A Man in Christ*, pp. 169,170.
28. *Redemption Accomplished and Applied*, p. 170.
29. D. A. Carson, *Jesus and His Friends* (Leicester, Inter-Varsity Press, 1986), p. 90.
30. Carson, pp. 98-9.
31. John Calvin, *St John 11–21* (Edinburgh, The Saint Andrew Press, 1972), p. 97.
32. J. C. Ryle, *Expository Thoughts on John*, vol. 3 (Edinburgh, The Banner of Truth Trust, 1987), p. 116.
33. A. W. Tozer, *The Root of the Righteous* (Harrisburg, PA, Christian Publications Inc., 1955), pp. 75-6.
34. Marcus Dods, *The Gospel of St John*, vol. II (London, Hodder & Stoughton, n.d.), pp. 188, 189-190.
35. Louis Berkhof, *Systematic Theology* (London, The Banner of Truth Trust, 1963), p. 449.
36. See, for example, the sermon 'Public Worship to be Preferred before Private' in *The Works of David Clarkson*, III (Edinburgh, The Banner of Truth Trust, 1991), pp. 187-209.
37. John Murray, 'The Nature and Unity of the Church', *Collected Writings*, vol. 2 (Edinburgh, The Banner of Truth Trust, 1977), p. 334.
38. John Murray, 'Nature and Unity of the Church', p. 335.
39. J. C. Ryle, *Charges and Addresses* (Edinburgh, The Banner of Truth Trust, 1978), p. 297.
40. John Calvin, *Institutes of the Christian Religion* (London, SCM Press, 1961), III.viii.1.
41. Ferguson, *The Holy Spirit*, p. 172.
42. Westminster Shorter Catechism, 37.
43. Heidelberg Catechism, 1.